The World of Jay Leno

The World of
Jay Leno

His Humor and His Life

by Bill Adler
and Bruce Cassiday

A Birch Lane Press Book
Published by Carol Publishing Group

A Birch Lane Press Book
Published by Carol Publishing Group
Birch Lane Press is a registered trademark of Carol Communications, Inc.
Editorial Offices: 600 Madison Avenue, New York, N.Y. 10022
Sales and Distribution Offices: 120 Enterprise Avenue, Secaucus, N.J. 07094
In Canada: Canadian Manda Group, P.O. Box 920, Station U, Toronto,
Ontario M8Z 5P9
Queries regarding rights and permissions should be addressed to
Carol Publishing Group, 600 Madison Avenue, New York, N.Y. 10022.

Carol Publishing Group books are available at special discounts for bulk
purchases, for sales promotions, fund-raising, or educational purposes.
Special editions can be created to specifications. For details, contact
Special Sales Department, Carol Publishing Group, 120 Enterprise Avenue,
Secaucus, N.J. 07094.

Manufactured in the United States of America

10 9 8 7 6 5 4 3 2 1

Library of Congress Cataloging-in-Publication Data

Adler, Bill.
    The world of Jay Leno : his humor and his life / by Bill Adler and
Bruce Cassiday.
        p. cm.
    "A Birch Lane Press book."
    ISBN 1-55972-145-6
    1. Leno, Jay. 2. Comedians—United States—Biography.
  I. Cassiday, Bruce. II. Title.
PN2287.L432A62   1992
792.7'028'092—dc20
    [B]   92-29925
                                                        CIP

Contents

The World of Jay Leno

1

"Perfect"

J AY LENO IS PERFECT. He doesn't drink, smoke cigarettes, take drugs, or chase women, and he's
happy. He is what every mother wants her son
to be. And he is a rich and successful comedian.
What more could you ask for? With his squeaky-clean image,
he's Hollywood's answer to political correctness.

When he tells jokes with his high-pitched voice and his
ironically prognathous jaw, the audience can't help but crack
up. Leno comes across onstage like Frankenstein's monster
telling jokes with Mickey Mouse's voice box. In fact a Hollywood casting director once told Leno he was too "fright-
ening" for children to look at.

That shows how much those peabrains know. Now Frankenstein's monster/Mickey Mouse/Leno is laughing all the
way to the bank. But he holds no grudges against the tin-pot
Hollywood pooh-bahs who raked his career over the coals
when he first tried to crash Hollywood.

Leno is the avatar of the American dream. He's the perfect guy who comes from the perfect middle-class family and
lands the perfect job. He is dedicated to his career and has a
strong work ethic. In fact one of Leno's first cable specials
was styled "Jay Leno and the American Dream."

His parents are solidly middle class and knew little hardship in life. His father, Angelo, is Italian American and was an insurance salesman who frequently told jokes at sales meetings or when he served as master of ceremonies at company banquets. Jay's mother, a housewife, was born Catherine Muir, in Scotland.

Leno didn't get his sobriquet "Jay" until grade school. At birth on April 28, 1950, he was named James Douglas Muir Leno in New Rochelle, New York—"Jamie" to his family. Jay is ten years younger than his brother, Patrick, a lawyer who is now in insurance.

Leno admires his parents and has only good things to say about them. He was happy as a kid and claims his type of comedy—delivered without malice—is a result of his upbringing.

"I come from the kind of family where my mom ironed my socks," he says. "In case my shoe ever fell off, people would know I came from a good family."

His family moved from New Rochelle to Andover, Massachusetts, in 1959, when Jay was nine years old. He spent the rest of his adolescence in Andover.

He liked his father so much he wanted to grow up and be just like him. "I just assumed I'd always be some sort of gregarious salesman who knew a joke to emcee birthday parties."

Leno can't remember an unhappy day in his life and recalls his childhood with fondness. In junior high school he enjoyed flushing tennis balls down toilets and detonating cherry bombs in urinals.

"But these were not career moves," he has joked. His favorite prank was to sneak into the girls' bathroom and pour water through the Kotex dispenser. He admitted to an interviewer in 1986 that he "liked watching that metal machine expand and tear apart from the napkins' absorbing the water. It was very funny." A pause. "It would be a good ad for Kotex."

Even as a baby Leno was a joker. His wife, Mavis, once described a baby picture of Jay: "His face is just popping with mischief. He had curly black hair and almond-shaped eyes. You can see that there is some kind of forceful personality just dying to emerge." Interestingly enough, Jay's mother was forty-one when she bore him.

The genetic theory is that Leno inherited his chin and blue eyes from his Scottish mother and his dark hair and coloring from his Italian father. In 1985, on a tour of Europe, Leno took his mother back to Scotland for the first time in sixty years, where they visited Greenock, the town where she was born.

Greenock is a respectably sized town, located no more than seven miles from one of the most famous "lochs" in all of Scotland—Loch Lomond—and not so very far from Glasgow.

Catherine Leno took her grown son for a stroll through the town, recalling whatever details she could remember from the past. And to Leno's shock, she kept pointing out local Scotsmen who looked startlingly similar to him!

About Leno's smashing success in show business, his mother remarked, "It took him a while to get to where he is, but that was the way I wanted it. I didn't want him pushed, pushed, pushed."

Leno recalls that his mother said to him, "'There's a time to be funny and a time to be serious'"—sounding like a reprise of Ecclesiastes—"and of course I never could figure when the time to be funny was. No one ever *said* when that time was."

The time for Jay to be funny, it turned out, was *all* the time.

"He was always funny, Jay was," his mother confirmed. "He was always joking as a child. But we thought he was going to be a salesman like his father."

More than just a joker, though, "He was always helpful,

too," Catherine Leno said. "If a car was broken down on the road, he'd get out and help. He had such a happy disposition."

As she said, she always thought he was going to be a salesman. Or a mechanic. "Once I told him that, as an investment, he should buy a service station. That way he'd have plenty of room to store more cars." She paused to reflect. "What's he got out there in Beverly Hills? Twenty cars?" In fact, he owns nineteen vintage automobiles and forty motorcycles.

She laughed. "The only time I ever saw Jay get mad was over his car, if anybody borrowed his car. He's got all those cars out there now, but *we* can't drive them."

When his mother wanted to use a car during a recent visit to the Coast, Leno told her, "Mother, I'll *rent* you a car."

Leno's mother and father don't mind being used by their son for a good laugh on national television. "People that know me," Catherine said, "they love it when Jay talks about his mother and father."

When Leno returns home on a visit, he's just like somebody from the neighborhood again. "He says, 'Hello, Ma, how are you?' and he's off to see his buddies."

"A year ago," Leno recalled, "I went to see a guy I grew up with, and his mom actually said to me, 'Well, what are you going to do when this show business thing slows down? You going to come back our way?'"

Leno, outraged: "I mean, I'm the host of the 'Tonight Show,' but they think if that doesn't work, there's the rubber plant in town, the sneaker factory."

Big sigh.

As a school kid, Leno, eager for laughs in South Elementary in Andover, used to allow other kids to slam him on the head with a hammer so he could prove how hard his head was. Leno later recalled the experience, saying, "Ow! My head would hurt so much."

Leno remembers the first time he told a grown-up joke. There was a typical class discussion about Robin Hood and his merry men.

The teacher said, "You know, people were very cruel back then. They killed people by boiling them in oil."

Jay raised his hand and protested. "But they couldn't boil Tuck." Pause. "He was a friar."

Leno: "That was the first time I think I ever told a joke joke, a grown-up joke. And I remember thinking, 'Hmmm, that's an interesting reaction.' And since then I've always been able to remember everything I said, good or bad, and the reaction it got. I was never particularly good at remembering names or spelling or adding, but I could always remember what made people laugh."

The truth of the matter is that Leno was a somewhat indifferent student. He was once analyzed as mildly dyslexic. One guidance counselor even suggested that it would be best for him to drop out of public school.

He was the proverbial class clown who was at his best when cutting up for laughs. The result for Jay, however, was more than an occasional lonely trip to the principal's office.

Earl Simon, Leno's fifth-grade teacher, had this to say on his spring report card:

"If James used the effort toward his studies that he uses to be humorous, he'd be an A student." But Simon could see the talent there. He continued: "I hope he never loses his talent to make people chuckle."

At the age of fourteen, Jay, a child of the automobile culture, bought his first vehicle, a 1934 Ford pickup truck. During his high school years he got a job working at Wilmington Ford as a car washer, then later worked at a Boston Ford dealership. One day he dropped a hubcap from a load he was carrying. A supervisor saw the accident and fired him. Leno wrote a letter to Henry Ford II protesting the firing and asserting that he loved Fords. Ford called Leno's old boss, who summoned Leno to his office and rehired him.

Since that time, legend has it, Leno has always personally answered every letter sent to him.

He also held a job for a while at a nearby McDonald's. There, he used to give away bags of food. His friends would come in, and he'd say, "Ten burgers, eight fries, thirty shakes—that will be a quarter." Every kid who worked there gave away pounds of the stuff.

Once Tom, the manager, came in and said, "We lost twenty-five thousand dollars last month. What happened here?"

Leno, with a straight face: "Oh, gosh, I must have given the last guy the wrong change."

At McDonald's, Leno got his first taste of show biz. They conducted a talent competition among the McDonald's shops in the area, and Tom told Leno, "You're the funniest one. Why don't you put a skit together?" Leno agreed. His monologue won him a camera for first prize.

When he graduated from Andover High School in 1968, he listed his possible future career in the yearbook as "retired millionaire."

After high school he entered Bentley College in Waltham, but after a year transferred to Emerson College in Boston. College bored Leno. He spent more time at Boston bars, practicing his stand-up comedy routines. He would go into a saloon and tell the owner, "I'm a comedian."

"Get out of here," was the knee-jerk response.

Leno would slap a fifty-dollar bill down on the bar. "Just let me tell some jokes, and if people leave or I embarrass the customers, you can keep the fifty."

Most of the managers were pretty decent to Leno. Even when they might not think him uproariously funny, they would always give him back his fifty dollars. But once in a while a manager would say:

"Hey. You're a funny kid. Why don't you come in next week, and we'll pass the hat?"

At Emerson he tried out for the school's comedy workshop—at the same time he was working gigs at night in Boston professionally—but was *rejected.*

Nevertheless he emceed campus talent shows, which starred guitar players whining about life being over at the age of nineteen.

Introducing these acts, he said "a lot of stupid stuff," but occasionally he would come up with something that made people laugh. When that happened, he made sure he said *that* again. After six or seven months of experimentation, he discovered that he had a semblance of a routine in hand.

Though he wasn't taking any formal comedy classes at Emerson, clearly he was studying for the future.

His parents never wanted him to go in that direction. "There was no master plan," Leno said. "My parents thought that just to go to college at all was amazing. Their advice was finish college, get your degree, and you can always teach if you can't find something else." Resounding support for a show-biz career it was not.

Soon Leno graduated from bars with their fifty-buck entry fees to joints in Boston's so-called Combat Zone, the city's red-light district.

Among the many places he had to work were sleaze joints like the Teddy Bear Lounge, the Kit Kat Club, and a dive called Nude—just Nude. One cheap club that didn't have enough letters to spell out his name on the marquee billed him as "the talented Mr. No."

At that time Leno was, by his own admission, no more than "a stupid college kid with long hair and glasses." It wasn't easy back then. He'd get up on the stage and do typical sociopolitical stuff left over from the sixties, usually winding up with the line: "Hey, Nixon. What a jerk! Heh-heh-heh."

Knocking Nixon was always good for a laugh, but the rest of his material rarely was. His surroundings were unbelievable. In one Boston "club" he worked in front of a pantomime scene that was at best weird. Directly behind him two nude women took continuous sponge baths in a pair of enormous champagne glasses.

From the posters outside, Leno learned that their names were Lili Pagan and Ineeda Mann. Actually, they were hardworking show-biz professionals in their forties. Their main claim to fame was that they had gotten into "the theater" in the good old days right after World War II.

If anything, they exhibited true maternal instincts toward Leno. One night a heckler began cursing at Leno in the middle of his act, effectively shutting down his routine.

One of the naked women climbed out of her giant champagne glass, ambled over, and gave the guy a hard punch in the nose. Broke it! The heckler went down like a bowling pin and lay on the floor, out cold.

Leno can't remember if his savior was Lili Pagan or Ineeda Mann, but when she surveyed the wreckage on the floor, she came back onstage and chirped at Leno:

"Go ahead, dearie. Do your act."

Relieved, Leno took the microphone, said, "Thank you," and launched into his best material ever. "Naaaah, Nixon— what a jerk!"

In recalling those slime-bucket clubs he played in when he was starting out, Leno never asks for sympathy for having had to work under such conditions. Instead, the motherly instincts of the nude strippers reminded him of home. "It was like traveling with my mom."

Once when he was twenty-two years old, he recalled making up in a dressing room shared with six nude women. It was not, to Leno, a negative experience at all. "I was a college student and I was making thirty, forty bucks a night. It was great! And the strippers were very protective."

"Stay away from Joey," they would warn him. "He's a dealer."

Not all the strippers were that maternal. One of them came on to him one evening with a cheery, "Hey, kid, how about getting it together later?"

Apparently Leno was not at all averse to trying out this new lifestyle after his routine, for he agreed to look her up.

"When I came back," he said, "there she was, her leg up on a chair, totally naked. There *I* was in my best jacket and nice tie, carrying a box of candy and a bunch of flowers. I was so *naive!*"

In those years it was necessary for Leno to reach deep down within himself to take up the challenge of the life he had chosen to lead. Well, why not? His friends were making two dollars an hour waiting on tables in restaurants, and here he was making forty dollars a night onstage with the well-rounded Ineeda Mann in her birthday suit.

Leno sounded like a poor imitation of Mort Sahl at these dumps with his political jokes. "Nixon, what a jerk! . . ." Audiences weren't impressed. Instead of clapping, they flipped lighted cigarettes at him and guffawed as he tried to dodge the missiles. These were the only laughs Leno got those nights. "Awful places," he reminisced.

Actually, Leno claims he likes hecklers, especially if they're any good at insulting him. "I'm not adversarial onstage. I actually like a good heckler who can keep pace and make the show funnier. But heckling isn't always that cerebral." Or that successful.

He met a lot of Neanderthals in his early years. Like in Revere Beach, outside Boston, where another cigarette-throwing incident occurred. The owner warned him to wear old clothes his first time there. Leno protested. "I want to look nice." The owner understood but pointed out that there were a lot of wise guys in the audience who thought it was the epitome of practical joking to use an entertainer as an ashtray once he was in place doing his act. A closer look would have revealed to Leno that the man had telltale burn marks on his jacket.

That night, as Leno went through his routine, the customers in the audience would wait until their cigarettes were smoked down to an inch or so and ready to throw away. Then they would take a hefty drag on them, get the ashes flaming, and toss the fireballs toward Leno.

Some of the hot missiles bounced off his cheeks; others landed on his jacket; still others stuck in his hair—which began singeing and casting a stench into the air.

All around him the laughter welled up: "Har-har-har!" The laughs were there, but obviously not where Leno had intended them to be. "I don't know how this custom originated," he said, "but it was like one of those Indian trial-by-fire things. Tough club."

Undoubtedly, Leno has lived through his share of horror stories on the nightclub circuit. One club he played in was called the Mine Shaft. If anything, it was worse than a real honest-to-goodness mine shaft. As a running gag, members of the audience wore phony miner's lamps on their heads—a kind of travesty of an eye-ear-nose-and-throat doctor's light probe. Leno had to perform his act in the minelike murk while a group of strippers pranced around on the stage behind him, exhibiting their wares to the flickering light of the miner's lamps. He was forced to stand off to one side in the semidark, doing his material like some latter-day Diogenes in futile search of an honest man. "Nobody could see me when I was talking," Leno recalled, "and nobody cared about what I was saying anyway. And when I looked out over the audience, all I could see was a bunch of lights glowing on everybody's heads."

Even when he moved up a notch or two, the customers at the Nameless Coffeehouse, the Sword in the Stone, and the Orson Welles Theater Café paid little heed to Jay Leno.

And then came a break. He opened one night at Lennie's, a jazz club located on the Massachusetts Turnpike. It was what people in the trade call an "A room."

Lennie Sogoloff—he and Leno are good friends to this day—used to bring in all the big jazz names to play at his North Shore Jazz Room, popularly known by Lennie's name.

In 1972, Sogoloff ran an advertisement for comedians to participate in what he termed "Monday-night hoots" or "open-mike shows"—supplementing the concerts of his jazz greats. Leno saw the ad and nerved himself up enough to drop in and audition.

"Jay Leno showed up," Sogoloff recalled. "He had granny glasses, an Afro, jeans, and the whole sixties look. The audition was like a scene in an old Warner Brothers movie."

Sogoloff sized him up, life repeating art. "What do you do, kid?"

"I'm a comic."

"So—make me laugh."

About thirty seconds into the routine, Sogoloff cracked up.

Leno: "He made me house comic!"

Lennie's featured a lot of the jazz stars such as Stan Getz, Mose Allison, Ahmed Jamal, Buddy Rich. On the night Leno opened, according to a story related by Tom Shales in the *Washington Post,* the crowd had become restless waiting for Buddy Rich, the famous drummer, the guy they had paid their money to see.

When Leno came into the club, a woman was on the stage singing, but the audience was getting unruly.

"Boooo! Get off! You're a slut!"

Finally the woman had had enough, gagged, and ran off in tears. At that point the audience started to settle down.

"All right! Yeah! Good riddance! Hey! We want Buddy!"

By now the emcee was a bit shaken, but at a signal from

Sogoloff, he put on a fragile grin and held up his hand for silence.

"We've got a bright young comedian!" he announced.

The audience wasn't buying *that*. "Boooo!"

The emcee was undaunted. He announced Leno's name. Somebody in the crowd stood up and shouted back, "We hate him!"

Leno: "Now, I had never appeared anywhere in this type of place. How could they hate me?" Squaring his shoulders in defiance, Leno strode out on the stage.

"Thank you very much, great to be here," Leno said.

"Booooo! Booooo!"

There were catcalls and whistling and stomping. Then a husky guy out in the front shouted loudly, "Hey, get Buddy out here or I'm going to smash your face!"

"Well, sir," Leno started to say, sizing up the heckler, whom he termed a "kind of Mafia guy."

"Get him out here right now or I'm going to smash your face!" the Mafia guy repeated.

If Leno is of any sociopolitical persuasion, he is the ultimate pacifist. "I figured, I'll try to be friends with this guy," Leno said.

"So, where you from?" he asked with a show-biz smile. The guy leaped at Leno and smashed him to the floor. Blood was seeping out of his scalp, and Sogoloff walked over.

"Come on," he urged Leno. "Get up and finish."

Leno looked around him, dazed. A couple was sitting about ten feet from him, but apparently they had not even seen the scuffle. If they had, they were neither impressed nor depressed.

Dizzy and in pain, Leno tried to struggle back to his feet. Two burly patrons were now holding on to the Mafia guy so he couldn't hit Leno again. The would-be comedian staggered into the spotlight and finally managed to get through his act.

He got his twenty-five dollars from Sogoloff. As soon as he was paid, his agent was there waiting for his commission of two dollars and fifty cents.

"That was the funniest thing," Leno noted to Shales ruefully. "I had to break a five to give him his cut!"

Some punch line.

2

The Early Years

LENO GRADUATED—if "graduated" is the proper word—from Boston strip joints to comedy clubs such as the Bitter End and Catch a Rising Star in New York City. Perhaps "lap-dissolved" would better describe his transition. He frequently visited New York while he was working as a part-time mechanic and auto deliveryman for a Rolls-Royce and Mercedes-Benz repair shop. Whenever he would deliver a car to New York, he made it a point to stay there and perform at one of the comedy clubs.

In New York he met up-and-coming young comedians: Robert Klein, Freddie Prinze, David Brenner, among others. They all advised him to move to Manhattan and pursue a comedy career there. At that time there weren't a lot of aspiring comics at these comedy clubs, so there wasn't all that much competition at the auditions.

At Catch a Rising Star, according to Leno, only two of them showed up for an audition one day—Leno and Freddie Prinze. It was as easy for Leno to work these clubs as it was later on for him to work Vegas and the "Tonight Show." Of his New York experiences Leno said: "Getting on was easy."

His first appearance on a real New York stage was at the Bitter End in New York, early in the seventies, while he was still going to Emerson College. He even remembered the first joke he told then, which was memorable for all the wrong reasons and went like this:

"You could do anything in your room at college. You could smoke pot, live in a coed dorm, have a girl. But you couldn't have"—pause—"a hot plate!" Leno immediately went into an imitation of a stuffy college dean on the telephone. "Mrs. Leno? This is the dean. We've got your son Jay—yes, it was on suspicion of soup. The lab boys say it was *definitely* Campbell's cream of mushroom."

Looking back on that gag later, Leno shrugged expressively. "Hey! I was only in the business a *week.*"

His later success in New York was slow in coming. He drove to New York twenty-four times before finally getting the call at the Original Improvisation, a stand-up graveyard for aspiring comics. He was still making deliveries for the Boston Rolls-Royce/Mercedes-Benz dealership. The other comedians got used to seeing him pull up in front of the Improv in a different Rolls each night.

Peter Tauber, a free-lance writer, wrote a story about Jay Leno for the *New York Times Magazine* in 1989. Tauber was an aspiring stand-up comedian in those days—and met Leno when he was on his way up in Manhattan. Tauber described him in these words:

"I am obliged to admit that I have known Jay Leno for years. I first met him in 1973 outside of the Original Improvisation nightclub on Forty-fourth Street and Ninth Avenue in New York. He was twenty-three, a bushy-haired kid in wire-rimmed glasses who wanted to be a stand-up comic, as did I for the six months or so I lasted."

Tauber notes that he did not really notice the "legendary jaw" and instead thought Leno favored the late Elvis Presley. "His most extraordinary feature," Tauber wrote, "was his aquamarine eyes."

What impressed Tauber the most was not Leno's physical

appearance or even his manner of telling jokes, but rather his against-the-grain character.

"He didn't smoke, drink, take drugs, tell jokes that demeaned any gender or ethnic group. He was, most other comics agreed, just a nice and funny guy who liked to talk offstage about books he'd read."

In 1973, after his graduation from Emerson College, Leno made a number of trips to the West Coast to work in the Los Angeles clubs, but his career never caught fire out there, and he would always return undiscouraged to the more familiar milieu of Boston and New York.

A year later, Leno's act at the Bitter End garnered praise from *Variety*. The reviewer lauded his impression of Elvis Presley singing Hamlet's soliloquy.

Leno maintains that he *did* have some jokes then—some very bad ones, such as this:

"I remember a joke I used to do—terrible joke—about the new male hygiene spray called Umpire, for men with foul balls. That was the joke. Just terrible, awful."

It was at the Bitter End that a party of his relatives came to visit him one night, at least according to a Dick Lochte interview in *Playboy* magazine. The story seems almost too good to be true—suspiciously like one of Leno's early routines about his family. Nevertheless for biographical purposes it bears study.

According to the interview, the owner of the Bitter End had told Leno that he could come back on a Tuesday, working for nothing, as was the custom. Naturally, the excited Leno told his parents and they agreed to form a support group for his big act.

The Bitter End at that time was an in place for young people who wore their hair loose and their jeans tight. It was an herbal-tea, joint-smoking place, trendy, exclusive, sparsely frequented.

Leno's relatives began arriving before he went on—

"Uncle Lou with the big hat," as Leno identified him, his grandmother "with the aluminum walker," about ninety at the time—and other aunts and uncles. Out of sight, Leno listened to their chatter about "Jay Leno"—with his grandmother crying out and clapping in time: "Jamie ona da stage. Jamie ona da stage."

Once up in front of the audience, Leno suddenly froze. Here was his family, watching him, and all he had in the way of material was "sophomoric, dirty jokes." All he could do was hem and haw, come up with a couple of off-the-wall standards that had the merit at least of being clean, and bow out, exiting in great haste. But to great applause. As for his relatives, they vanished—"maybe seven minutes after getting there, emptying the place for the next act."

Real or apocryphal, the story certainly brought to life the times at which Leno began practicing his art, the places in which he worked, and the lifestyle of that era.

Although there were some low points in Leno's career when he began it, success—albeit not stardom—came easily to him, and he is the first to say so. Once he felt confident about his career as a comedian, he admitted his easy early life was what made his outward-appearing persona so *nice.*

Oddly enough, he solidified his image of Mr. Nice Guy during his stint in New York nightclubs—not exactly the town one would consider the greatest gestating arena for consideration or politeness in any human being.

"I guess I'm nice," he said recently. "I have no reason not to be. Things have always gone fairly well for me. The real trick in show business is to find something you do well and just do it."

Leno has now been around long enough to have made a few motion pictures and a few television sitcoms, but he still prefers stand-up comedy to acting in front of a camera. He feels people come to hear him tell jokes. And that's enough for him. It's a good living that makes him feel fulfilled.

"I don't want to be on a game show just to be on TV." Leno considers himself a product—a valuable product. That's what the public wants to buy, and not an appearance of a cipher on some silly game show.

The ease of the life of a comedian appeals to Leno. In what other business can a person get up in front of a crowd, gab for an hour, and get paid big bucks?

"If you start playing only in selected places, pretty soon you lose touch," he warns. "I've seen a few comedians who were funny fifteen years ago and are still doing Nixon impressions and jokes about the women's liberation movement."

Of course, these guys are out of it. Leno equates a comedian's career with an athlete's, the object of the comedian being to get up to the plate as many times as possible before losing the ability to hit home runs.

Leno is not out to make enemies. If someone writes him a letter attacking his jokes, he will call up and find out what made that person so irate. He explained one such incident in detail.

"I did a joke one night when the movie *The Last Temptation of Christ* came out. I said a group of fundamentalists wanted to buy the movie back from the producers for ten million dollars to destroy it because they felt it was morally offensive. And that Warner Brothers was trying to contact the same group to see if they wanted to do *Caddyshack II*."

Soon after that, Leno received a letter, neatly typed, two pages long, that began:

"Dear Mr. Leno: Your recent five-minute attack on our Lord Jesus Christ . . . ," and went on to say, "I used to like you, and I had tickets to see you, but I tore them up and threw them away." There was more, all about Leno's attack on the Lord.

Leno telephoned the woman who had written the letter, and it turned out that she had not seen the show at all. A friend of hers who did see it had told the letter writer that Leno had done a whole monologue about Jesus.

"The problem is that people don't listen. When I'm on Carson, it's eleven-thirty at night, people are half-asleep, and there are certain things you just can't say because they won't hear you correctly."

One might wonder why Leno is so concerned about how people view him. If his explanation is true, his motivation is purely a financial one: he does not do racist, sexist, or ethnic jokes that might offend people because, in his words, "it's a marketing decision, not a moral one. I find I get more laughs working clean."

Every day Leno watches comedians who do raunchy, sexist, racist stuff. After *his* act—a clean one—people come up to him and say, "Thank you." Making other people happy is his greatest fulfillment.

He's the type of guy who helps little old ladies across the street. Boarding a plane, "nice-guy" Leno once pushed his way in front of a frail woman in a wheelchair. She waved him on. "Oh, go ahead, dearie." That did it!

Leno: "I felt like the guy on the *Titanic* who puts on a dress so he can get in the life raft first."

Never again, he vowed, would he act like a boor or a person with special privileges. And since then he has stuck to that commitment.

Leno is not an egomaniac. Nor does he ever exhibit an aura of false modesty about the amount of money he makes. The self-absorbed Hollywood mentality is not for Leno. "I don't need ten guys feverishly sorting through bags of M&M's because I don't like green ones," Leno pointed out. "I just want a glass of water and a stool."

Though Leno was working the New York club circuit and hanging out with comedian friends in Manhattan, he was still anchored in Boston. Plenty of his show-biz associates— Billy Crystal, Richard Lewis, Freddie Prinze, Jimmie

Walker—would visit him at his Andover apartment, staying overnight, or for the weekend.

The Andover digs was a kind of "fabled spot," according to Barbara Isaacs of the *Rochester* (New York) *Democrat and Chronicle*, a shrine for a lot of comics, since so many of them, then up-and-coming, crashed there when they were playing Boston and the Bay Area.

It was house guest Freddie Prinze who purchased a gun one day—for what reason was never really made clear. Anyway, he brought the weapon over to Leno's apartment and began fooling around with it, to the horror of Leno and those who were there with him.

To this day Leno cannot recall the incident without a shudder. According to him, Prinze shot off about three hundred rounds of ammo right there in the living room. Leno said the comedian blew a huge hole between the living room and the bedroom. You could see right through the wall! Some comedian.

The landlord must have been out of town at the time.

According to Richard Lewis, Freddie Prinze's actions with the gun came as no surprise—and certainly left remarkably little change in the digs, in spite of the hole in the wall. The place, according to Lewis, was never what anyone could remotely term "neat." He claimed a corn chip became permanently embedded in his back when he lay on the floor one night. The carpeting was half an inch deep in snack food.

Leno: "That's just classic persnickety Lewis." (NB: Bostonians pronounce *pernickety* with an extra *s*.) "Lewis washes his hands forty times a day," Leno went on. "The apartment could *never* be clean enough for him."

Before Leno went on to New York, he played at the Cellar Door in Washington, D.C. There he opened the act for Muddy Waters. What he experienced there made the Boston strip joints in his past look tame by comparison.

He walked out onstage and said, "Hi, everybody."

Instantly a customer came up behind him with a ketchup bottle. *Bang!* He cracked Leno a hard one on the head with it. Leno keeled over, out cold. Everybody in the audience thought it was Leno's humorous impression of a guy getting mugged in the capital city. Ha, ha, ha.

Soon after that Leno was in New York where he worked gigs in Greenwich Village or anywhere else he could get himself booked. He admitted later that he was a lousy performer in those days. He would clutch the mike with both hands, reel back and forth, and take a country mile to reach the punch line.

"I used to work Café Wha? in the Village," he recalled. Some guy would get up and read a poem: "Stop your war machine. Thank you." That would be the poem! Then somebody would say, "Okay, now we've got a guy who's going to do some comedy for you. Hit it, Jay."

Leno would get up. "Hey, Nixon. What a jerk!" Big pause. And that was his act. "It wasn't *anything*," he admitted later. "I was just stupid."

Rahsaan Roland Kirk was one of the jazz musicians whom Leno had met at Lennie Sogoloff's place on the Massachusetts Turnpike. Leno ran into him again at the Main Point in Philadelphia some time later.

Kirk was blind, black, and very, very talented. Besides that, he had a marvelous sense of humor. He could play tunes through his nose and do all kinds of weird tricks. But his main claim to fame was as a rap artist. Back then he was way ahead of his time with a special "black nationalist rap" routine he charmed his peers with.

Leno met Kirk backstage at the Main Point before going on. Kirk agreed to introduce him to the crowd when he finished his act. As the black musician started in on his diatribe against all whiteys trying to subvert all blacks, Leno glanced out into the audience.

The room was mostly full of males wearing shades, along

with beetle-browed frowns, many of them beginning to mutter under their breaths "Get whitey" and "Right on!" and so forth.

At the end of his routine, Kirk, true to his promise, announced:

"I'd like to introduce you to a *brother* who's going to entertain you!" He paused for effect. "And here he is! *Brother* Jay Leno!"

Stunned at the appellation *brother*, Leno stepped cautiously out in front of the crowd. To—*dead*—silence. For a moment. Then there was a sudden little murmur of discontent that began to rustle across the room toward him in a menacing manner.

Leno surveyed the almost universally black audience, grinned faintly, and waved a friendly hand at Kirk. "Hey," he said. "Maybe you haven't *noticed*." Pause. "Rahsaan's . . . blind!"

The statement was so outrageous that even the diehards in the crowd burst out into spontaneous laughter at the remark. Leno had them in the palm of his hand after that.

But he didn't always succeed in turning disaster into triumph. Take the time he endured a debacle at a college where he was harassed not by guys in shades but by well-educated, well-groomed students.

As Leno recalled it for Tom Shales of the *Washington Post*, he was in a small upstate New York town about eight hard-driving hours from Boston. A sorority was paying him twenty-five bucks a night for a three-night gig.

"Okay, you're in Study Hall C at nine tonight," he was told when he arrived.

"So I go to Study Hall C," Leno told Shales. "There's a thumbtack with an index card on the door: 'Tonight: Jay Leno.' Doesn't say what I do or anything."

Once inside at nine o'clock, Leno was confronted with a roomful of kids sitting there studying. Not a sound otherwise. Then six women appeared—members of the sorority that had hired him.

"Okay," they called out to the students. "Everybody! We have a comedy show here!"

Somebody in the group groaned. "Hey, shut up! We have a test!"

But the women were undeterred. One of them handed Leno a microphone and a speaker. In one hand he held the microphone and in the other the speaker, aiming it at whomever he was talking to. In that awkward fashion, he managed about forty-five minutes of material, while the students continued putting their hands over their ears and shouting out:

"Why don't you just get out of here and go home? You're not funny. You're—*stupid!*"

At the end of the first night, Leno searched out the women who had hired him and told them, "Listen, girls, this isn't going to work out."

"Oh?" one of them responded aggressively. "Well, we're going to call your agent and tell him you're *uncooperative!*"

Confronted with that threat, Leno agreed to perform the next night. Once again he was obliged to enter Study Room C. It was filled with the same kids he had seen the night before!

"We saw you last night!" someone shouted. "Shut up, you're not funny. Why don't you go home?"

The third night he was sitting in the cafeteria eating before the show, and several of the sorority women walked by him. One of them saw him and turned up her nose, whispering to her companions, "There's that jerk that thinks he's a comedian."

Leno sighed in retrospect. He told Shales, "They may still be there!"

Welcome to Comedy Hell.

But that was fun and games compared to a gig he did over in New Jersey a short time later. There he was hired by a man who wanted him to pretend to be someone named Bob Carlyle, director of sales for an unnamed company.

As Bob Carlyle, director of sales, he would simply do his routine, wrap it up, and leave the audience rolling in the aisles.

Leno appeared at the scheduled place for his act and faced about seventy-five people who looked like shoe salesmen or middle executives of some kind. He did his stand-up and was received as well as could reasonably be expected—considering that he had assumed the ID of Bob Carlyle, director of sales, and not that of entertainer.

There was a smattering of applause. The man who had hired him bounded up onto the stage and held up his hands for silence.

"Okay!" he shouted. "That, of course, was *not* my director of sales, but Jay Leno—a professional comedian!"

He then explained that he had assembled them all to receive, absolutely free, a special dispenser kit. The audience, Leno learned later, was composed of Liggett Rexall representatives. And the kit contained something called Fresh'n—a brand-new product.

"This product will revolutionize personal hygiene!"

"What is it?" somebody had the temerity to call out.

Well, it was a moist towelette used to combat—here he picked up a packet and read from the label—"embarrassing rectal odor."

They were like Wet-Naps! Ugh.

Immediately the hall began to empty. No one seemed to want the free dispenser kits. No one even wanted to *think* about them.

"Wait!" the man shouted. "I've got two hundred thousand of these in my warehouse. I want you to have one free—to take home. Please! Take a dozen! Put them in your stores! No charge! Please!" Leno rushed out with the rest of the deserters.

"There was a midway in Minnesota," Leno recalled, "where I stood doing my gig between the pig-elephant tent and the half-woman/half-snake exhibit. The half-woman/ half-snake had a picture of Liz Taylor pasted over a snake. But *inside* the tent, there was a horrible fetus with a snake attached to it. You had to pay a quarter to see it. It was—"

Worse than the fetus and snake was the scratchy mike Leno was stuck with. Competing with the screams of kids, the wheezing of the carousel's steam calliope, and the screeches of the women on the Ferris wheel, Leno did the best he could—which, he had to admit later, was not very good.

One level lower than the half-woman/half-snake exhibit was the time Leno auditioned in the early seventies for the second Jack Paar show, called "Jack Paar Tonight." He was waiting outside with the rest of the hopefuls when the talent coordinator strolled by and caught sight of him. With a jaundiced eye he surveyed Leno disdainfully. "Is *that* the suit you're going to wear on the show?"

Leno nodded. "Yeah."

The talent coordinator shook his head. "Listen. Go on home. This isn't for you."

Another problem concomitant with tacky clubs is the seedy hotels you have to put up at where you do the show. These places can be more nightmarish than the clubs themselves. Leno stayed at some of these places when he started his comic career, and probably the most disgusting of all was an old, really ancient, hotel in Cincinnati. They charged him three dollars a night, and even at that cut rate the room was overpriced. Leno's had a toilet in the middle of it.

He woke up one night in the wee small hours. It was dark, but the light from the corridor came in under the door and showed a stream of water flowing into the room. He got up and looked out.

An old man was placidly urinating in the hallway against

the door. "What are you doing?" Leno asked, although *that* was most obvious.

The old man made a face. "Oh! I'm sorry. I *always* urinate on this door."

Leno stared at the man and at the door. The door was all rotten in the lower corner. The old man was right. It was his door.

Not many people know this, but Leno used to work with a comic partner named Gene Braunstein, who later became a story editor on TV's "Who's the Boss?" The partnership broke up in the late sixties and Leno joined an improv group called Fresh Fruit Cocktail. He actually beat out Braunstein for the job. The Fresh Fruit Cocktail played the Playboy Club and several other joints. Leno loathed the experience. He could not stand depending on other people in the group: "I never liked team sports as a kid. I never understood the concept."

Then there was the time he opened for Rare Earth at George Washington University, in Washington, D.C. Rare Earth was a singing group that had made it with a big pop single, "Get Ready." They were tops at the time. It was 1973, and Leno was twenty-three years old.

"I came down to the university," Leno said, "and the audience is all neighborhood kids from the area—mostly teenagers, mostly boys about fifteen years old." When Leno entered the gymnasium that had been hastily refurbished to serve as an auditorium, the manager of Rare Earth pulled him aside.

"Hey, listen," he warned. "Rare Earth's got a lot of expensive equipment on the stage. You can't use the stage. You've got to stand on the gym floor."

That didn't bother Leno exactly. There wasn't much of a stage anyway. So he agreed and opened there on the floor, facing an audience that was crowded in all around him. Leno was looking right into their grinning faces at eye level. The cord of the mike snaked along the floor and then vanished underfoot.

"Anybody here from Boston?" Leno asked cheerfully.

Wrong city. Somebody in the crowd jerked the cord and the mike flew out of Leno's hand, bouncing along the floor off through the audience—boom, boom, boom, the sound monstrously amplified in the echoing confines of the gym.

"Hey!" yelled Leno, taking off and running through the laughing teenagers, trying to chase the wire and get the microphone back.

Someone laughed. "Hey, bro—what's happening?"

"Give me that!" Leno shouted back. "Give me that mike!"

He traced the cord through the crowd, and when he got to the end of it, the mike was gone. That was the end of his act.

Before he left, Leno sought out the manager for his pay. "The mike is your responsibility," the manager told him.

"They docked me seventy-five dollars out of my pay for it. It was all so stupid. It was the most *horrible* job. I mean, unbelievable. But that's show biz!"

This particular episode sounds like a Rodney Dangerfield routine. You can see Dangerfield sweating and tugging at his tie, saying, "I get no respect."

As for Leno, despite his long love affair with comedy, he found some things about the life so distasteful and discouraging that it was sometimes soul-destroying.

In Buffalo, New York, he was doing a TV gig on "A.M. Buffalo" sometime in the early seventies. The other featured players on the show were a number of so-called authentic Pygmy dancers. They wore bones in their noses and grass skirts over their tummies. And carried huge spears taller than they were. They didn't have a word of English and paid no attention to Leno, but grunted at each other and waved their hands in the air.

The show's talent coordinator suddenly walked into the green room. Picture the scene: a band of grass-skirted, spear-bearing Pygmies babbling in some weird tongue; a solitary male comedian dressed in casuals. And so the talent coordinator took this all in, blinked, and called out in the usual stentorian tones of talent coordinators:

"Mr. Lenooooo?"

Leno was about to respond. But the coordinator couldn't wait to sink in the hook.

"Which one is Mr. Leno?"

No one knows for sure whether the real Mr. Leno stood up or not.

One night in 1974, as Bill Barol in *Newsweek* has it, Jay Leno was sitting down in front of his television set in his Andover apartment, watching the "Tonight Show Starring Johnny Carson," when an unnerving thing happened.

There was a comic on the show who was simply awful. More to be pitied than blamed. Leno realized that if this downer had got booked on the Carson show, there was certainly a chance for Jay Leno in Los Angeles.

He decided to take a long shot at a miracle. Left all his personal belongings behind him. Opened the door and told his neighbors, "Good-bye. I'm going to Hollywood. You want anything, take it." Carried nothing but a pocketful of change and a lightly packed flight bag. Strode out of his digs. Caught the next red-eye to L.A. And changed his life forever.

People's Jack McCallum cites a different motivation for the transplant. He has Jay Leno muttering to himself something like this: "If I stay here in Boston, I'm going to acquire all the things that make life comfortable. Then I'll never get a real shot at the top of the comedy pyramid."

A Leno observer later examined the seeming recklessness of his move and decided it was a firmly rooted character trait.

Hadn't Leno always worked it so that he could never, ever make a living doing anything but comedy? Hadn't he always avoided taking a regular job? Hadn't he always left himself in a loose position, so that no matter what happened to him, he could always get onstage immediately?

Whatever, he traded Boston and New York for Los Angeles—quite likely because the "Tonight Show" had just moved there from Manhattan in May 1972. From that day on he was going to call the Left Coast his home. That would be the place his career would catch fire—or failing that, the place where he might find a modicum of success in some area of his beloved comedy business.

3

Late Night With Jay

L ENO FLEW TO LOS ANGELES in 1974. With his limited resources, he opted to sleep on other comics' couches rather than pay the inflated West Coast rents. A few times he even slept in the backseat of the 1955 Buick Roadmaster he bought as soon as he got there.

He admitted his first months in the City of the Angels were a little rough. "You'd meet a kindly waitress who would let you use the toilet, and then you'd drive across town to use someone else's shower." Pause. "It's handy training—if you ever have to hide out from the police."

Leno was twenty-four years old at the time. "When I landed in L.A., I hitched a ride out to the Sunset Strip. Then I walked and walked to the Comedy Store and hung out there until it opened. I went on that night, and luckily they liked me."

Comedians didn't get paid to work there, but it was fun, as Leno explained to *People*'s Patti Corcoran. "I like to look upon those first few months as my 'romantic' period."

The transplant from coast to coast did not cause him to become an instant success. His career did more fizzling than skyrocketing for some time, although he did manage to become a regular at the Comedy Store and the local Improv.

Eventually, some years later, he also appeared on Mike Douglas's show, on Merv Griffin's, and on "Late Night with David Letterman."

Johnny Carson even showed up for Leno's act once at the Comedy Store in 1975 after Harvey Korman urged him to take a look at Leno. Carson, however, was not at all impressed.

"Johnny said that, yeah, it was funny, but there weren't enough jokes," Leno recalled ruefully.

Ticked off that Carson had seen him and rejected him, Leno pelted the "Tonight Show" host's car with eggs in the parking lot at the Comedy Store. It was not a good night for Leno—nor for Carson's car.

In spite of his feelings about Carson and what Carson had told him, Leno did not dismiss the "Tonight Show" host's rejection out of hand.

"I went home and watched the 'Tonight Show' religiously and realized that Johnny Carson was doing about fifteen to twenty jokes in the time I took to do four or five. He was right in what he had told me. I still feel badly that I egged his car." Pause. "But not much."

Carson's message *did* get through to Leno. "I realized then that the trick is to get as many jokes into the shortest space possible. Take that hour and a half of material you have and make it the funniest five minutes in the world."

It wasn't until March 2, 1977—*three years* after Leno had arrived on the West Coast—that he finally got the break he had been waiting for: a shot at the "Tonight Show."

It happened like this:

All sorts of comedians and entertainers continued to extol Leno's merits to Carson. Comic Steve Martin had caught Leno's act and liked it. He told his contacts at the "Tonight Show" that they should give Leno a try. Carson was still open to suggestions about his guest lists, and eventually the interest of others won him over.

"I'm very grateful to Steve Martin," Leno once told Dick Lochte. "I appeared on the 'Tonight Show' thanks to him, and he didn't know me from a hole in the wall."

From that day on, Leno vowed to hold out a helping hand to aspiring comedians. He has done whatever he could for them since. When he caught Dennis Miller for the first time on "Saturday Night Live," he recognized an admirable talent. He told everyone he could about him.

Leno: "You take care of one another in this business."

About the Carson guest shot, Leno pointed out that even though it was a real breakthrough for him, his life did not change overnight. The phones did not ring with agents trying to sign him up or mentioning job offers. If anything, there was little reaction to his initial appearance.

"When I did my first 'Tonight Show,' I did fine, sat down, the phone didn't ring, nothing particularly happened. I was always somebody who had to do a hundred shows instead of ten, and then people would say, 'Oh, there's some funny stuff.'"

As for his routine itself, Leno told "60 Minutes" in March 1992: "Your first 'Tonight Show' is kind of like your first girl, you know. I mean, it's real fast. It's over real quick. You weren't very good. But you never forget it. But you do know, you want to do it again. And do it better the next time."

He had to wait a long time to take the phone call that would summon him back to act as *host* for the "Tonight Show." Meanwhile, times were lean.

Leno did seven or eight more stints on the "Tonight Show" as a guest, but for some reason his routines got progressively worse. They were so bad that he wasn't invited back—*for eight years!*

Leno never fell passionately in love with L.A., either. "In Los Angeles," he explained, "you have all those dramatic types who introduce themselves, 'Hi, I'm Susan, and this is my *lover*, Bob.' My lover? Shut up! Why don't you just lie down and do it for us right now?''

But Leno never regretted his move to the West Coast. "I wasn't married. I had no family to raise. There was no reason to.''

Nevertheless, Leno never liked the fast life of the L.A. nightclub scene. He once said, "If God doesn't destroy Sunset Strip, He owes an apology to Sodom and Gomorrah.''

He also said, "I know people who finish their act and say, 'I've got to get drunk and have some sex in this town.' When I finish my act, I go back to my room and watch television, or I'll go out for pizza with a friend. I'm hopelessly American. If something doesn't come in a styrofoam box with a lid on it, I'm lost.''

It was tough working in L.A. initially. He didn't really find any kind of job security until comedian Jimmie Walker hired him late in 1974 as a comedy writer for the hit TV show "Good Times.''

It was at the Comedy Store in 1975 that Leno met David Letterman, who was to become Leno's biggest fan, and the real key to Leno's later success.

The first meeting occurred one day when Leno was watching the tryouts from his vantage spot at the rear of the Comedy Store—as it had become his habit to do. He was always looking for good new comedians with good new slants on material and new insights on the craft of comedy that he might be able to incorporate for himself. That day, though, there were a lot of untried raw performers who were obviously nervous and unsure of themselves.

Then suddenly there was this guy—Leno found out later he was from Indiana—who pulled up into the parking lot out back in a pickup truck. When he climbed out, Leno saw that he had a beard and actually resembled Dinty Moore—Jiggs's sidekick in the old *Bringing Up Father* cartoon strip, the buddy with whom Jiggs usually ended up in the last panel on a floating I beam dipping into a lunch pail of corned beef and cabbage.

The auditions continued to drone on and on. Leno had decided to leave when finally the Dinty Moore look-alike appeared on the stage and began doing material that was certainly *not* like the stand-up stuff the Comedy Store was used to.

Leno's ears pricked up. He was entranced by the soft, persuasive voice. And then the import of the material worked its wiles on him. Later on he tried to remember exactly what Letterman had been talking about. The closest he could come to it was a short line or two like this: "We are diametrically opposed to the use of orphans as yardage markers on driving ranges."

The man was definitely an original. Leno sensed that his outlook was so much more advanced than that of the others trying out that he was a distinct standout in the world of stand-up. His delivery was impeccable, quiet and controlled, cool and savvy. His material was highly sophisticated, intellectually superior, and subtly memorable.

He was so good that Leno went over and sought out the newcomer after his bit. He introduced himself and told Letterman, "Gee! You've got great stuff."

According to Letterman, Jay Leno had a "huge influence" on *his* career. "After I saw Jay work for the first time in 1975, I said, 'Oh, *that's* the way it's supposed to be done.' What I was then was Jay Leno on a very bad night."

Letterman said of Leno, "He was head and shoulders above anybody else." And he admitted, "I patterned much of what I did on what I saw him do. It's no surprise to any of us that he's gotten so successful. I think everybody was surprised that it took him a little longer. The first night I saw him, I thought the next day he was going to be a huge star."

These were not great times for Leno, any more than they

were for Letterman, but the two of them continued to plug away at their craft. Leno was probably the hardest working of the whole fraternity of comics.

When he found that the magic portals of television would not open up for him, Leno simply return to the medium that had welcomed him when he started out—the nightclub and live-show circuit. In the years that followed, he averaged between two-hundred and fifty to three-hundred live comedy gigs a year, more than any other contemporary comedian. And his audiences *loved* him.

His wife, Mavis, disagrees with other Leno observers that her husband worked hard because he enjoyed it. He worked hard because he *had* to. Talking about the time between Leno's guest shots on Carson and his guest-host gigs—a long eight years—she said, "Jay went through a long desert space between being good enough to open shows for other performers and being good enough to open for himself."

In contrast, his contemporaries Billy Crystal and Robin Williams both became successful practically overnight.

"The main way to do that," Mavis went on, "is by getting a starring role in a TV show. But Jay was not considered good-looking, and his comedy isn't 'wacky.'"

Once Leno almost won a part on a TV show, but he was finally told he was too ugly. "They are not going to let me in the front door," he said to Mavis, "so I'll have to go around the back. It will just take me longer."

Unlike Leno, Letterman *did* get a real break not too long after he had started showing up at the Comedy Store. And it was his good fortune that finally helped turn Leno's faltering career around.

In 1982, Letterman premiered as the newest and most original of the late-night talk-show hosts. What was even more original about the show was that "Late Night with David Letterman" was not a "night" show per se, but a "wee hours of the morning" show. It started at twelve-thirty A.M., *after* the "Tonight Show" ended, and went on until one-thirty.

From the start, the night-owl show was a success, although its Nielsens were nothing to write home about. Letterman brought an incredible wackiness and offbeat humor to those early-morning hours. The show was once described as being "to TV talk shows what Salvador Dalí was to traditional painting."

Everything was just slightly out of focus. For the motion picture *Reds*, for example, Letterman interviewed a dentist—an obvious gibe at the typical talk-show "expert" usually on view. He even held an in-depth interview in a deadpan manner with an automobile mechanic about "celebrities and their auto repairs."

One night the cast and guests had an elevator race in the building. Another time they strapped a live camera to the back of a romping chimpanzee, which they turned loose in the studio.

But the stunt that got the most telephone calls was the "360-degree show"—in which the picture on the television tube made one complete rotation during the hour, so that halfway through the show, Letterman and his guests appeared upside down.

The perfect showcase for Jay Leno's humor. Leno fit like a hand in the glove of Letterman's flaky talk-show concept. More and more he found himself sitting beside Letterman, chatting through the early-morning hours during his periodic visits to New York City. With Letterman, Leno was able to make the most of what he had.

"Dave's show did everything for me," Leno acknowledged. "The show is geared well to what I do, in the sense that a lot of jokes I do there wouldn't work on other shows, because the host wouldn't have the rapport I have with David and wouldn't know what I'm talking about."

As mentioned, during the seventies, Leno was doing

about three hundred gigs per year in every state of the union—a business schedule judged by his peers to be the most backbreaking in the business. But for Jay Leno it proved to be mother's milk.

Letterman explained that the reason he kept inviting Leno back on his show was because of the audience's always enthusiastic response to him. As Letterman put it, "Jay Leno is the funniest comedian working today."

"David and I essentially come from the same place, comedically, so we can have a good time," was the way Leno phrased it.

As he told Dean Johnson of the *Boston Herald*, "I can be more aggressive on Dave's show than on the 'Tonight Show.' I can be loud and pick on Dave, really annoy him, which is a lot of fun. Like, when I eat on his show, it drives him crazy." Grinning. "It's *fun* watching him squirm."

Leno would never, ever *think* of eating on the Carson show. Nor could he ever get up the nerve to do the "Hey, Johnny—*nice tie!*" bit with the raja of late-night talk. In fact, Leno was never able to master the impulse to call Carson anything but "Mr. Carson," which seemed to him to be a fawning, cringing attitude, reducing him to some kind of teenybopper begging for movie money. He never got to the point where he could say "Johnny."

But with Letterman it was always different. The two of them got to know each other well. "When you do Letterman's show," Leno went on, "you get recognized by comedy fanatics—college students, and people who go to comedy nightclubs a lot. When you do the 'Tonight Show,' you get recognized in the frozen-foods section of the supermarket when you go shopping."

It was Letterman's special brand of humor that entranced Leno:

"He was great from the start, with very clever stuff. Never any cheap shots or Dolly Parton jokes."

Leno calls Letterman "an armchair quarterback," and himself "a foot soldier of comedy."

On the Letterman show, Leno found that he could act wilder than anywhere else and have the audience splitting its collective sides. On the Carson show he had to be more restrained. Maybe that was the reason he took that involuntary eight-year hiatus. His routine simply wasn't properly on target there.

And then, quite unexpectedly, the "Tonight Show" had asked him back. He began to click more than he had before. It appeared that he was actually building a following. Naturally, his continued success on the "Letterman" show had helped him immeasurably.

It was on September 6, 1986, that Jay Leno was asked to serve as "guest host," thus putting a definite end to his "guest" appearances on the Carson show. Being a host added a new dimension to his act. He took to it like a duck takes to water.

To Leno, guest-hosting the Carson show was a cinch. He never bothered to study the notes researched by his production staff on the guests he was to interview. Leno always preferred to work spontaneously with them.

An interesting and revealing confrontation occurred in 1988 between Leno and Fred de Cordova, the executive producer of the "Tonight Show," over Leno's carelessness with valuable research material.

"Young man!" de Cordova snapped. In his seventies, he was a most unlikely first sergeant. "Have you read your notes for tonight?"

Leno came to attention as best he could, looking unconcerned and very much laid-back, California style. "Yes, sir! All set!"

Somehow the certainty did not *quite* come through. De Cordova: "Now, look me in the eye and say that!"

Leno looked him in the eye, then began treading water

like a nonswimmer about to go down for the third time. "Oh, the *notes!* Uh, yeah, yeah. Got a little busy in here today, boss. Didn't have much of a chance to take a look at them. Uh, I think they, uh, they . . . *fell behind the couch!* That's what happened!"

Why should he study his notes when he always had the audience in stitches when he was ad-libbing?

Leno once tried to explain the difference between his actions as guest host on the "Tonight Show" and as guest on the "Letterman" show. It had to do with the various roles he was playing. On the "Tonight Show," he was required to serve a totally different function than on "Letterman." When he was guest host he had to be the calming influence after his stand-up was over and he was interviewing guests. It was he who had to maintain control, with the guests allowed to horse around at will.

First he would come on with ten minutes of fast stuff for the stand-up. Then he would shift gears and moderate his energy level. As host, in his Hyde-to-Jekyll transformation, he would then be almost the opposite from his stand-up role. He would wind up straight, proper, and subdued—the epitome of congeniality.

On the "Letterman" show he came on as guest only. That meant he had no reason to tone down. It was up to Letterman to be a calming influence on him. Leno did not have to maintain control at all—he could do anything. His energy level did not have to be lowered at any time he was on camera.

Leno once pointed out the logical flaw in the habit network moguls have of hiring frenetic deejays to act as hosts of television shows. The flaw is built into the idea. A deejay is frantic because his job as disc jockey is to send his listeners into orbit *before* a record or video begins to play. Once the music is on, the performance takes over and the energy level tends to subside. But on a talk show, the deejay doesn't usually act to control the interview—if anything, the deejay tends to become both guest *and* host. After twenty minutes of hyperventilating wit, and half-wit, the viewer has had it.

The lesson, of course, is to be aware always of the nature of the performance. As stand-up—zingers. As host—a kinder, gentler mood.

Leno's breakthrough year *was* 1986. Following his frequent visits to the Letterman show, he played to a sold-out crowd at New York's Carnegie Hall. He would also host his first hour-long comedy special, "Jay Leno and the American Dream," which aired on cable's Showtime. He then signed a multiyear contract with NBC.

That same year Johnny Carson picked Leno as one of two permanent guest hosts for the "Tonight Show." Gary Shandling, who later quit to do his own show on cable, was the other.

About their dual schedule, Leno quipped, "I hosted most Mondays and a bunch of nights without vowels in them or something." Actually, he hosted the show on Tuesday night during the football season so he did not have to go up against ABC's "Monday Night Football."

Leno once tried to explain the sputtering way his career always went, even after his first "Tonight Show." "I wasn't 'one of the guys.' When Freddie Prinze did the 'Tonight Show,' boom! His first one! Producers called, and he had a series the next day. And a few other people did it that way, too."

Leno was always, if nothing else, philosophical. "I was dropped from the Morris Agency twice, and from ICM twice. They said, 'There's no future. You have to have a hook. You have to be the guy from outer space or the wacky guy.' But I don't hold any grudge."

Letterman showcased Leno's talents better than the "Tonight Show" at first. Leno put in a monthly appearance there. As already explained, Letterman would play the straight man to Leno's wild man. Letterman is much more blunt and demanding than Leno, who tends to be self-effacing.

"I don't think Dave has a mean streak in him," Leno observed. "I've never seen him do anything mean. He's just honest. I've just seen him speak his mind. He'll say to a guest, 'Well, that's completely stupid, and you're an idiot.' But he believes that! I believe it, too, but I probably wouldn't *say* it."

Leno admitted he has toned down his material since his first appearances on the Letterman show. Its admittedly dangerous edge was skillfully honed. He was then accused, however, of becoming soft and fluffy.

In response to this criticism, which appeared in the July 1991 issue of *Vanity Fair*, Leno countered with the following explanation:

"When I was doing Letterman, the material was a bit more left of center. When you do the 'Tonight Show,' you essentially do one-liners about what's gone on that day. And being on once every six weeks with Letterman is different from being on every night of the week.

"And yes, it is more bland now. As I *do* the show now, obviously I'm a guest in somebody else's house. So, you don't criticize. You say, 'Oh, this is fine,' and you work within that framework." There was, obviously, method in Leno's politeness.

Once a woman with an acne-scarred face wrote to him to object to his joke about a photograph of Manuel Noriega on the "Tonight Show." In the photo, according to Leno, Noriega was standing there holding a big machete. His comment was, "Judging by the looks of his face, he's also been shaving with this thing."

Leno called the woman to apologize. "You know, I was making fun of the *man* and his personality. I didn't mean that he had acne so much as that he was an ugly man." Leno had felt obligated to explain his joke because he didn't want to hurt the woman's feelings.

When Leno guest-hosted the "Tonight Show," as he said, he was a comedian "from eleven-thirty to ten to twelve"—during the stand-up and the first sitdown, before the guests were introduced.

"Then I stop and I listen to what people say. I'm not trying to be funny all the time. I don't want to get into that lampshade mentality." And so he shifted gears mentally after his stand-up.

These were the reasons he came across so differently on the "Tonight Show" from the way he did on the later-in-the-night Letterman show. Leno also said that he preferred hosting the "Tonight Show" to appearing on it as a guest. He always found it more relaxing to be host:

"I don't really have a whole lot of interest in my own career from the standpoint of talking about it. I just ask people questions, the way I do when I'm sitting down at an airport waiting for a plane, something I do a lot."

Leno admitted owing his success on TV to Letterman. After Leno was appointed Johnny Carson's successor on the "Tonight Show" in 1991, he said:

"I don't think I would have this job if it wasn't for David. I think Dave does the brightest stuff on TV, and I'm always annoyed when I watch other talk shows and they lift, verbatim, chunks that Dave has made famous. I always say, 'Oh, come on! That's a rip-off!'"

Even as late as April 1992, Leno was being attacked for his tendency to neuter out into a kind of blancmange comedian—a would-be satirist without the cutting edge he had displayed back when he was known as the "Bruce Springsteen of comedy."

"I never thought those shock comedians could last just being antigay or antiwomen," he told Digby Diehl in *TV Guide*, referring to Andrew Dice Clay and his type of comedy. "Maybe some of it was funny the first time around, but where do you go from there? Who do you hate the next time?"

To which comment Diehl responded in print: "Aw, c'mon, Jay. Nobody's asking you to become Clay, but among comedians, don't nice guys finish last?"

Then Diehl shifted into editorial gear: "The great tradition of American humor—from Mark Twain through Will Rogers to Lenny Bruce—has conspired to sting the smug and shake up the complacent." Diehl wound up with a rhetorical question: "Is Leno becoming too cautious to gore our sacred cows?"

4

"The Tonight Show With Jay Leno"

F OR MONTHS there had been conflicting rumors floating about the television industry. Johnny Carson was going to quit. Johnny Carson would *never* quit. Carson was signing a ten-year contract. Carson was going on a two-nights-a-week schedule. And so on and so forth.

On February 11, 1991, the *New York Post* published a bold story with the headline: THERE GOES JOHNNY. The subhead read: "NBC Looking to Dump Carson for Jay Leno."

But who believed the *Post*, anyway?

Answer: lots of people.

The story, written by Bill Hoffmann and Timothy McDarrah, contained a series of quotes from a "source" speaking for "top honchos" at the NBC network. The gist: NBC "wants Carson to sign off" so he can be replaced by Jay Leno. The reason? Jay Leno "pulls in a younger audience more attractive to advertisers."

"Out of loyalty," the source said, "they [the NBC heads] want to give him [Carson] one more year because it'll be his thirtieth anniversary on the air."

The story then went off into amusing byways probing side issues, one a speculation that the people at NBC were more concerned about who was going to tell Carson he was through than with any actual plans for the future. The network seemed to be simultaneously moving in two directions. A spokesperson scoffed at the idea of Carson's retirement, pointing out that fifteen years before this there were rumors that Carson was out.

"Let the record show," said Curt Block at NBC, "that Johnny Carson will be the one who decides when he leaves the show." The idea behind *that* seemed to be a fairly strong nudge to Carson, indicating that if he did not get the hint and take action himself, the ax would then be swung by one of the top brass.

For more than three months nothing happened. Nothing was said.

On May 23, something did happen. Carson appeared at a press conference at Carnegie Hall and told the world that May 22, 1992, would be his last night on the "Tonight Show." He did not mention the name of any successor. NBC did, on the very next day. It was indeed exactly as the *Post* story had predicted: Jay Leno would take over after Carson's retirement.

The announcement did not come as a shock to Leno fans, but it did to David Letterman's.

When *he* heard the news, he was said to be "fit to be tied," according to the news media. Letterman immediately denied it. "I've never been tied in my life," he claimed, twisting the word into a typically esoteric Letterman double entendre. "There's not a man alive who can tie me!"

He added, "I couldn't be happier. I think Jay'll do a fine job." Letterman did admit he wanted the job: "I'd like to at least be considered for the gig. If it were offered to me, I would certainly take it."

Carson didn't want to get into any dispute between Letterman and Leno. Carson said he liked both of them, but added:

"Dave has been on the air for ten years, so he has a good

track record. I didn't know how badly he wanted it. I heard he was disappointed. But it was NBC's call." Apparently Carson had no say in the matter. "NBC didn't ask me one way or the other. NBC never discussed it with me."

Leno denied that he and Letterman were battling each other for the same job. "This is the greatest thing that ever could happen," Leno admitted exuberantly. "It's the same as an actor winning an Academy Award. It's the best job in show business."

And: "This is a job I always wanted, that I always thought it would be neat to have. But I can remember casting people, people in television, saying to me, 'It will never go to someone who looks like you. Nor will it go to a Jewish guy. The show is too mainstream for that.'"

Associates who were close to Carson maintained that Carson was surprised at the network's decision and felt that Letterman should have been offered the slot over Leno.

A *New York Post* follow-up story repeated that NBC really had wanted Carson to quit before May 22, 1992, but had decided to give in to his decision as to the day. It was pointed out that Leno had been getting better demographics recently than Carson. People close to the action believed it was actually Leno's backers who leaked the demographic story to the press in order to promote Leno's career and take Carson down a notch.

Leno never denied that his followers had planted the offending demographics story. What he did say—somewhat lamely—was that he had never believed in demographics anyway: "If you look at the numbers, you see that the 'Tonight Show' has always been double what the other shows have been in the same time period, except when the Persian Gulf War was on and they watched 'Nightline.'"

Nor did Leno pretend that he did not campaign vigorously for the job. It was known that he made a habit of schmoozing with NBC affiliates all over the country, taking time out during his long and wide-ranging swings back and forth over the landscape to charm every executive he could possibly meet. He also reminded all the NBC brass during these swings of his enormous popularity with the public in general, using the data of his backbreaking schedule of three-hundred-odd gigs a year as proof of his ability to woo and hold viewers.

Leno felt that he landed the show because of his extensive and continuous traveling back and forth across the face of the land: "I've played every city in the country—including Alaska—at least once. I've worked with network affiliates, giving interviews, helping them do spots, selling tickets. I think I have them to thank.

"And I take it as a compliment that people can't place me geographically."

What he meant was that he would frequently see people who would ask him, "Aren't you from Grand Rapids? I saw you play there." The same for Sioux City, perhaps, or Colorado Springs.

Leno: "I don't think I would have gotten this job if I'd gone through the normal testing and screening process."

He figured the reason was simply that he was what might be termed a "good soldier."

"When I go somewhere, it's to stay. It's a bit like living together for five years and then deciding to get married. I like things that have a sense of history."

The president of NBC Entertainment, Warren Littlefield, agreed with Leno's comment. "Leno has proven extremely popular with the late-night audience, and we are confident that the show will continue its late-night dominance for many, many years."

But of course, in the end, Leno clearly expressed his views that getting the show was no *vital* thing. "It never really made any difference to me," he said. "I like doing what I'm doing"—just writing jokes and being a comedian. "I've always sort of been happy at every stage. I don't mean that to sound political."

The truth of the matter was that the plot of the coup d'état at the "Tonight Show" orchestrated by Gentle Jay Leno did not fit his carefully formulated image. The real story of the plot would have made him look like a conniving upstart who couldn't wait to bite the hand that had been feeding him guest-host shots on the "Tonight Show."

Defending himself, Leno had nothing but good words for Carson and his durable popularity. "I remember in the early seventies, Johnny was king, and then in the midseventies, oh, some bad stories, and then 1980, the cover of *Rolling Stone*, 'the greatest,' and then in 1985 when Letterman was on, 'Oh, Johnny is old hat,' and blah blah. And now he's king again."

Letterman, on the other hand, never did this sort of political glad-handing across the countryside. How could he hope to beat out Leno for Carson's job simply by doing his *Late Night* show? Leno had a shrewder understanding of the political machinations in Hollywood than Letterman and knew how to promote himself to the men in suits who commanded the power structure of big-time show business.

Leno tried to downgrade the existence of a so-called grab for Carson's job. "This is not a case of any sort of struggle going on. I've just been sitting in the wings, and when Johnny said he wanted to go, great! They called me, and I said, 'Yeah, fine, let's do it.' This isn't some sort of competition or power-struggle thing."

It was Leno's rather shaky position that he did not know Letterman wanted Carson's job until he read about it after he had already signed the contract. "I must admit I did not have a clue till it hit the papers that Dave had designs on the job," Leno noted, all sincerity and candor. "I never heard it mentioned. It was never brought up." Critics have pointed out that Letterman had admitted setting his sights on the job in published interviews years before. Maybe Leno never read them.

Leno stated that there were no hard feelings between him and Letterman because of NBC's decision to go with Leno. In fact, according to Leno, "Dave called to congratulate me and stuff, and we're friends. And I think it's more the way it was handled. If two people live together and you tell your parents you're going to get married next Tuesday, that's not the same as saying you got married last Tuesday."

When Leno read a *National Enquirer* article that stated Letterman had "vowed to ruin" Leno's show out of resentment at him, Leno quipped, "Well, if there's anything Dave does, it's vow. When I speak to Dave, it's a word he often uses: 'I vow!' I can just *see* Letterman vowing."

Leno conceded that Letterman's anger created a thorny interval in their normally friendly relationship. "It's not nearly as awkward as these things could be, were we not good friends. I sincerely think that if I didn't get the job, I would have wanted it to go to Dave, and I think he thinks the other way around.

"It's like two guys get in the ring, you know? You can be friends."

In the *Seattle Times*, David N. Rosenthal offered one explanation in a June 3, 1991, story of why NBC favored Leno over Letterman. The network, he said, would be cutting its own throat if it chose Letterman for the eleven-thirty P.M. spot. Carson's audience would refuse to watch Letterman. That same audience would, however, stick with Leno. The reason was simple: Johnny Carson's audience, Rosenthal theorized, did not find Letterman funny.

Why not? Because Letterman was rough with his guests, making fun of anyone who wasn't as hip as he. Leno, on the other hand, ridiculed only the rich and the powerful. Leno would never rag the average Joe who comprised most of his audience. Leno fell somewhere between Carson's era of "old show biz" and Letterman's era of "anti–show biz."

The upshot of the whole Carson-Leno-Letterman rhubarb occurred when David Letterman appeared with Johnny Carson on the "Tonight Show" on Friday, August 30, 1991. Jay Leno was not present—except in spirit. Or in imago.

It was Carson who had the first word—and it was a memorable word at that, at least on national television.

Referring to Letterman's feelings about the choice of Leno to host the "Tonight Show," Carson looked at his guest and asked with a smile:

"Just how pissed off are you?"

Letterman let the gasps and chuckles at the use of that hardly ever heard phrase on national television die down before responding.

"You keep using language like that and you're going to find yourself out of a job," he admonished Carson.

"There were rumors you were going to bomb NBC," Carson responded.

Letterman gave what amounted to a smirk. "I hate waiting in line."

Then Letterman turned solemn. "I'm not angry. I'm not angry at NBC about this. I'm not angry at Jay Leno about this. I'm not angry at you or the 'Tonight Show' about this. Now if the network had come to me and said, 'Dave, we want you to have this show,' then a week later they said, 'Dave, we don't want you to have this show,' *then* I would have been angry. But I have a show and NBC can do whatever it wants to with this show."

Letterman then added the coup de grace. "Now, would I *like* to have this show? Oh, sure—yeah."

Carson: "Can you see yourself doing the 'Late Night' show twenty years from now?"

Letterman laughed heartily. Then he went into one of his

favorite comedic routines: a lengthy General Electric–bashing joke. GE, of course, owns NBC.

And that was the end of it.

Except for the buttering up Letterman did on his own show concerning the brouhaha.

"Before we continue," he said, "I think we should congratulate our friend Jay Leno for being selected as the host of the 'Tonight Show.' And the good news for *us* is, *we* get Stump the Band."

In the long run, it was the consensus in the entertainment business that NBC had played it pusillanimously safe by hiring Leno to supplant Carson. Leno would offend fewer people than Letterman would, and therefore, Leno would attract the larger audience and gain the most advertisers. Leno appealed to the ever-important Middle America in the "Tonight Show" demographics.

And that brought up some problems not only for the network, but for the newly anointed host and the people the new host would be booking for the show. One night Carson was chatting with his old friend Don Rickles—an actor and celebrity who had been a fixture of the "Tonight Show" for years—a record seventy-eight appearances at last count, according to *Time* magazine.

In his usual abrasive and witty style, Rickles was ribbing Carson about surrendering the seat he had so long occupied behind the desk there in beautiful Burbank's posh studios.

"So!" rasped Rickles. "What are you going to do now? Where are you going to go now?"

Long pause. There was laughter. That died down.

Carson looked Rickles square in the eye. "The question is, where are *you* going to go?"

More laughter. At Rickles's expense. The comedian got the point. Carson's audience would not necessarily be Leno's audience. Carson's guests would not necessarily be Leno's either.

Leno's ability to focus on his family as well as on politics gave him a somewhat wider appeal than Carson did.

"I would assume his [Leno's] chief popularity lies with the twenty-to-forty audience," said Steve Allen, the first "Tonight Show" host. "But I'm in my sixties and I certainly enjoy his work." In fact, Allen has nothing but praise for Leno. "I think he would have been just as successful twenty years earlier or twenty years into the future, for the simple reason that he is a likable, funny, witty fellow."

To fellow comedian Jerry Seinfeld, Leno is "Robocomic" because he is flawless. "I'm sure if you caught him at some unguarded moment, you would see a panel fall open on his chest to reveal wires and electrodes. He is Robocomic."

Art Buchwald said this about Leno: "He's a warm person and it comes through in his humor. Johnny Carson is not a warm person." He also preferred Leno's stance on the day's news. "Leno is a lot sharper than Carson, particularly in his political humor."

Mark Shields, a *Washington Post* columnist, and a fan of Leno's, wrote: "In 1988 [a national election year] he came close to Will Rogers. His monologues on politics are unequaled."

Shields thought he knew why. "It's the salt spray that gets up in the North Shore. If you grow up in Kentucky, you know all about whiskey and racehorses. If you grow up in Nashville, it's country-and-western music. In Massachusetts, it's politics. *The Last Hurrah*, remember, wasn't set in Santa Monica." Shields is originally from South Weymouth in the Bay Area and should know.

Kevin Rooney, another comedian friend of Leno's, backs up this view: "He'd be happy if he could do comedy as an eight-hour workday. He likes being a journeyman. Besides, he doesn't do normal stuff like have a cup of coffee or a cigarette or a beer."

The ghost of Will Rogers surfaced in another discussion

on the choice of Leno as "Tonight" host. Wilbur Hixon once taught history at Andover High School to Jay Leno. Back in 1967 he let Leno take over the class one day as a mock teacher.

"For forty minutes, he put on a show," Hixon recalled. "Everybody found something to laugh at. He didn't have to cross any lines to be funny." And he still doesn't, Hixon noted. "He hasn't changed. That's what's great. When I listen to him today, I'm proud because he has such insights into history and current events. He uses the headlines of the day just as Will Rogers did. He emulates him a bit."

Time magazine in its cover story on Jay Leno in March 1992 paralleled Jay to Will Rogers as well: "Will Rogers never met a man he didn't like; Leno wants to say he never met a man who didn't like him."

Back in the early seventies, a Boston promoter named Fred Taylor saw Jay Leno, but didn't think much of him then:

"In 1972, I wouldn't have given Leno a whole lot of odds on becoming a star. Material-wise, he was sharp. He was current-events savvy. The newspaper was his resource. But he was intellectually astute, not funny. He needed timing. He needed the body movements onstage. He needed to move from spoken-word funny to theatrical funny. I give him a whole lot of credit. For him, becoming a star was strictly a bootstrap operation."

Leno's reaction on getting the job he had always wanted was typical. He turned it into a one-liner. "This is probably the only job in the world where you get the job and they go, 'Okay, good! You'll be starting . . . in a year.'"

And later, on the show: "Johnny's leaving. Ed's leaving. Doc's leaving. I feel like that kid from *Home Alone.*"

In early 1991, when there was speculation that Jay Leno might someday be taking over the "Tonight Show," he was asked when he thought Carson would quit. Leno: "Roughly when Princess Margaret ascends the throne."

"I kind of got the 'Tonight Show' job the same way I've gotten everything else," Leno said in retrospect. "I was never someone who anybody got particularly excited about. I mean, I've been with all the major talent agencies and been dropped by all of them."

He was never the kind of act that people would speak of ecstatically: "Oh, you've got to see this kid, he's going to be the biggest thing ever!"

The agencies would always tell Leno: "You're not enough of this, you're not enough of that, you don't have a hook." But Leno would simply watch television and note that the people who remained reasonably popular were the ones who were never accepted in one specific direction or the other. Arthur Godfrey. Bob Newhart.

Leno laid his success to his own short attention span. "The nice thing about doing the 'Tonight Show' is that my attention span is about five minutes. And this is a show that is done in *real* time. There are no retakes. It's a lot like a nightclub. You walk in front of an audience, and you try out jokes. If they work, great. If they don't work, well, you try to do better tomorrow night.

"I also like the fact I can sit home and read the paper, look for material. Most comedians, as soon as they think of something, they want to tell people. They want to go down to the club tonight. Now with the 'Tonight Show,' I can just go on TV and say it."

Leno smiled. "Guests I may not *personally* like usually turn out to be better than I expected. Even the worst people can *seem* very nice when they're all dressed up. And reasonably polite."

About interviewing, Leno had this to say: "Doing interviews is easy. These people are here because they want to be, plugging a book or a movie or something. This isn't an in-depth, secret probing of their lives. We're here to entertain and I try to keep the guest comfortable. It's not a problem at all."

It was a long time in coming—the job on the "Tonight Show." "I have been lucky in being able to build my reputation gradually through my stints as a guest host. I've been able to *sneak* in."

What Leno meant was, he did not have NBC announcing, "He's the funniest, wackiest guy in America!" Or telling Leno, "Jay, you're weak with uneducated children between eleven and seventeen, and so we're going to bring on the Smurfs as guests to take care of that." He was able to come in as himself, full-blown.

Asked once about whom he might prefer as an on-air sidekick when he took over the show, Leno mused and said, "Pat Buttram comes to mind."

(NB: Buttram was the second banana in Gene Autry's old singing cowboy films.)

But it was difficult for Leno to make up his mind about "guest hosts" during his three weeks of vacation time each year. Should he have them or not?

"This is all so new that we haven't even thought about it," Leno admitted. "I don't want any other talk shows picking up on our ideas. I think that when I'm on vacation, we'll just do reruns. That'll amortize the product."

He decided that his solid booking at "Tonight" would not cut down *all* his outside engagements. "I'll continue to play clubs on the weekends while I host the 'Tonight Show,'" Leno said, "although I'll cut back on my travels somewhat. I've been on the road for twenty years. There's no place left to go!"

Art Buchwald pointed it out best when he said:

"For thirty years, Johnny Carson has been the barometer for national humor. We all have to watch the 'Tonight Show' to see what the American people are accepting. Now Jay Leno will be our national weatherman of humor."

As for Leno, he had an observation to make about that. "I like to think people will tune in, even out of curiosity—like at a train wreck."

5

"I'm Always Me"

STANDING IN THOSE boxy metallic suits, Gentle Jay always looks like a member of a Fuller Brush salesmen's convention. Nobody knows where Leno buys his suits. He claims he got a ten-years' supply from a door-to-door salesman, so he'll be wearing them for years to come. Leno is six feet tall and weighs 180 pounds. He wears his blow-dried, grizzled black hair in a brushed-back style. He has aquamarine blue eyes. His massive undershot jaw gives his wide face an imposing cast.

According to Letterman, the only difference between Leno onstage and off is that "Jay wears less makeup offstage."

You would never catch Carson the Clotheshorse wearing one of Leno's box jobs. Carson has a flashy, glitzy image. Leno's nice-guy look tones down the "Tonight Show."

People would write in to him all the time about his lousy wardrobe. They didn't like his ties. They didn't like his shirts. They didn't like his suits. They didn't like his shoes.

That brought a typical reaction from Leno. He blew up. He was annoyed that they were not interested in his jokes, whether or not *they* were any good. All they cared about was the way he *looked*.

58

The truth of the matter is, clothes mean little to Leno. Perhaps they mean *nothing*. He wears them only for his image. They are essentially no more than a kind of twentieth-century fig leaf to appease the prudes. "You really shouldn't show your genitals in public," Leno told *Playboy* magazine.

Patti Corcoran wrote in *People* magazine several years ago that "Jay Leno has no—absolutely no—taste in clothes. It's not a minority opinion. Just ask his friends."

She then quoted Dennis Miller, of "Saturday Night Live," on Leno's sartorial taste: "Those ties look like they were made in summer camp, like fabric ashtrays he's wearing around his neck."

David Letterman she quoted as saying, "I don't *get* his clothes. I just don't get it. I don't get the pushed-up sleeves, the luminescent ties."

Leno's friend Jerry Seinfeld made it all into a sort of joke: "He dresses like an Iranian disco owner."

According to Dana Kennedy of the Associated Press, even his *mother* has things to say about his clothing. "He can't *wait* to get the tuxedos off!" she complains. "He likes to go off and fool around with his motorcycles."

Kennedy says Catherine Leno frequently scolds him: "It's no wonder no one ever recognizes you on the street—you're always a mess!"

Leno is as nice offstage as he is on. As he tours across the country he helps people out. Once a man was harassing a woman in a shopping mall and Leno rushed up to the woman and, pretending to be her boyfriend, said, "Hello, dear." The harasser scampered away.

James Wolcott, a writer for *Vanity Fair*, called him "the officially sanctioned safety valve of the middle class, letting off just enough steam to release tension without upsetting too many apple carts."

There won't be any Mighty Carson Art Players now that Leno has assumed the helm of the "Tonight Show." Leno doesn't play other characters the way Carson did. No Maud Flickerts, Floyd R. Turbos, Carswells, Carnac the Magnificents, Faharishis, El Moldos, Art Ferns, or Aunt Blabbies. Leno plays only himself. He considers himself a comedian, not an actor.

"When I was a kid," Leno explained, "I used to like Laurel and Hardy because no matter where they were, they were always Laurel and Hardy. I mean, if you put them in the Renaissance or had them signing the Magna Carta, they were still Stan and Ollie. Their personalities were ingrained, and that made me laugh."

Being himself all the time makes Leno's inner life that much easier; he never has to switch gears. "I'm always me," he says. And that's the secret of his stability and endurance in a professional milieu in which instability and insubstantiality abound.

In his comic routines, Leno never uses devices. He admits that a device is good for some comics because it can propel a mediocre performer to the top in quick time. But there's a built-in flaw. "You're stuck with the thing. If you're the Wacky Guy from Space, you might get on Carson one or two times. But the third time, you're just a guy in a space suit telling jokes."

Like other long-lived comics, Leno does not profess to be doing anything *new*. Comedy is *old*; the best comedy is the same way now that it was in the court of Augustus Caesar, or on the Greek stage. Among Leno's favorites when he was growing up were Jack Benny, Johnny Carson, Alan King, Groucho Marx, Bob Newhart—ordinary-looking people who surprised him when they came out with amusing things.

"I never really enjoyed the put-on-a-dress school of comedy," Leno confesses. He likes high-toned humor and the people who can come up with witty sayings when they are just lounging around in somebody's living room munching Doritos and drinking soda pop.

What is refreshing about Leno is the fact that he used to write all of his own material, as opposed to Carson, whose material on the "Tonight Show" was crafted mostly by staff writers. Leno never used Carson's writing staff when he was doing his guest-host shots on Carson's show.

Of course now that Leno appears five nights a week as the permanent host, he needs a writing staff. It would be impossible for him to come up with funny material day after day.

One of his writers is an Orthodox rabbi, Marvin Silberman, from New Jersey, now a permanent resident of Los Angeles. From Philadelphia came Joe Maderus, an advertising executive, now also living in L.A. Leno has used several housewives scattered throughout the Midwest, but on a smaller scale than now. Of course there will be others hired and put on salary in the future.

For his once-a-week appearances on the show, Leno made it a habit to spend a week practicing. There is no way he can do this now that he must fill a five-night schedule.

But when he was in it more or less on his own, he could walk out onto the stage of the "Tonight Show" in front of the massive gray curtain (instead of the rainbow-colored one especially crafted for Carson) and come up with quips such as the one on the marvels of the Soviet engineering feat of Lenin's tomb:

"The vegetables are moldy, the meat is rancid, yet they keep their leaders fresh and crispy."

When the show's producer, Fred de Cordova, heard lines like those he could only say in wonder, "The really good ones make it look so easy, like they've been doing it forever."

Leno never ridicules women with his jokes and he rarely does jokes about sex or drugs. His image is so squeaky-clean he refuses to do beer commercials and has so far agreed to promote only one product—Doritos.

"I don't drink, smoke cigarettes, or take drugs. I'm probably the straightest guy I know. So I'm not going to help sell beer or tobacco," Leno was quoted as saying in the September 1989 *Cosmopolitan.* "I agreed to do Doritos because it's a tasty chip and because I've never seen six dead teenagers on the highway with empty bags of Doritos around. It's not an inherently destructive product." He has confessed to smoking a pipe once in a while. And he actually does like to eat Doritos.

On the other hand, he cannot make his refusal to do beer ads adamant enough. "I won't do beer ads. I don't think these beer companies should be trying to get your adults— which we all know means teenagers—to drink beer. I don't want some father to come to my show saying, 'My kid got killed because of your ad.' I draw the line at taking money for something I don't use."

He told one reporter that he had no intention of promoting any other products. "I have no interest in selling products that aren't American made. I don't perform in other countries; why should I sell their products? I intend to be very nationalistic when it comes to industrial America. Doritos are harmless. I mean, obviously, it's not an apple."

Despite his popularity as a regular middle-class guy, Leno claims his multimillionaire status hasn't turned his audience off. If anything, it may have built him up in some people's eyes.

Leno retains his middle-class roots and exploits them. Obviously he can afford expensive Brooks Brothers suits, but they would clash with his regular-guy image. The boxy metallic suits are his style. With Leno, what you see is what you get. And apparently, he wants his fans to know exactly what they are getting.

Nor is physical fitness a part of his image. He comes from the school that says that if you have time left over to exercise at the end of the day, you're really not working hard enough.

Leno firmly believes in the Puritan work ethic he learned from his parents.

He thinks his job in comedy is not to favor one political cause over another, but to expose the hypocrisy and idiocy of *all* politicians. He purposely dulls the edge of his sarcasm:

"Like the joke about Bush going to a baseball game, then going to Bermuda to fly a kite, then saying he won't eat broccoli. Hey, maybe Quayle can handle the job after all!"

Leno once confessed that he enjoys doing political material. Carson is the master of political comedy. Nobody could figure out *his* political slant at all. With him, the *joke* always came first. Jay emulates Carson's lead.

But not *too* much politics. Leno read Lyndon Johnson's biography and remembered an important point Johnson made. "Each handshake," Johnson wrote, "is worth two hundred and fifty votes."

"And it's true," Leno avers. For example, if someone came up to Leno and asked him for an autograph, and Leno responded with a quick and nasty, "Hey! Get away from me. Can't you see I'm busy?"—that story would reach two hundred and fifty people in no time. Besides that, the victim of Leno's sharp tongue would *repeat* that story for the rest of his life. "To everybody!" Leno says in dismay.

His hobby of collecting motorcycles and cars is also very middle class in its appeal. The average person quickly thinks of the guy down the street with his old Dodge up on blocks in the backyard. Leno has always liked to play around with cars and motorcycles.

Part of Leno's image is his work ethic. "I consider myself a good soldier. You go to work, you do the job—write joke, tell joke, get check—and the world will pretty much take care of itself."

Leno admits, "I love keeping busy, seeing things through. It's how I relax. People say, 'Oh, I'll bet you sit in your pool all day.' Well, I went and sat in my pool once and hated it. I felt like a leaf."

In keeping with Leno's nice-guy image, he won't go anywhere near drug jokes. You'll never hear any gags about Bolivian Marching Powder from him. He explained why to John McCollister for the *Saturday Evening Post.*

One night a friend of Leno's made a funny remark about drugs. Leno and everyone else laughed. The friend told Leno, "You should try that onstage."

Leno shook his head. "I don't do drug jokes."

"That's okay. Try it."

Leno forgot all about it. Then one night he was doing his act, and in a lull in the routine, he threw out the drug line that his friend had given him. It got a *big* laugh. Leno shrugged. He had been wrong.

Then, at the end of the show, Leno was hanging around the place and talking to the members of the audience. One of them came up to him and asked, "What was this thing you did about drugs? That doesn't sound like you." Pause. "Do you use drugs?"

Leno was taken aback. It was amazing to him that after ninety minutes of gab, this fan had picked out the one line that was *not* Leno's. Nor was this any big fan of his. He was just one of the guys.

And Leno made up his mind. Never again, he told himself, would he do something that was not a part of what he generally did. That is, he would stick to the character of himself that he had carefully and patiently molded through the years.

Leno once allowed, "I'm the same guy onstage and off. All that stuff about 'laughing on the inside, crying on the outside'—I don't get it." Leno had the aphorism reversed, but that made his point not only telling but humorous as well.

Even though he has a very good fix on his audience and

on its response to his humor, he sometimes comes up short at an unexpected reaction.

"I did this Barry Manilow joke in 1985." At the time a number of popular rock stars and entertainment biggies had decided to make a special album, dedicating the profits to the starving people in Ethiopia, which had just sustained the worst famine in its modern history.

"When I looked down the list of names on the *We Are the World* album," Leno said, "I didn't see Barry Manilow's there. I thought, 'Jeez, that's funny. He's a big star. Why isn't he on the album?'

"So I called the Ethiopian embassy."

Their response was: "Yo! We're not *that* hungry!"

Leno pointed out that when he did the bit on the Letterman show, the crowd went, "Woooo"—meaning they didn't like it at all.

"I said to them, 'Wait a minute. This is stupid. I made fun of Nancy Reagan, I made fun of President Reagan. I made fun of the United States of America. Everybody laughed. But I made fun of Barry Manilow, and you went 'Woooo'? I don't know. Are popular icons held in higher esteem than our country?"

Point well taken.

It's interesting to note that Gentle Jay took over the reins of the "Tonight Show" under the Bush administration, interesting because one of Bush's favorite political slogans was a "kinder and gentler America."

On the other hand, the glitzy Carson took over the "Tonight Show" when Kennedy became president and installed a modern-day Camelot in Washington. Kennedy and Carson both had swinging night lives at the time. Carson reflected the glitz of Camelot as much as Leno reflected the gentleness of the Bush administration.

Paradoxically, Leno has been dubbed the "thinking

man's comedian," as well as the "working man's comedian," thanks to his sophisticated political jokes on the one hand and his typically middle-American McDonald's jokes on the other.

Neal Karlen, a *Rolling Stone* writer, noted: "Leno refuses to lecture like Lenny Bruce, pontificate like Mort Sahl, or cop false anger like Eddie Murphy." In truth, this attitude tempers the bite of his political barbs.

In Leno's own words: "I would rather make fun of the corporation, or whatever it is that dehumanizes people, than make fun of people themselves. Nowadays you make fun of nuclear power, giant computers that send people nine-thousand-dollar phone bills; you laugh at that because here is a chance for the human spirit more or less to triumph over the machine. . . . It all comes down to good jokes. It all comes down to whether it's funny or not."

Corporations—or countries. For example: "My wife loves Europe, but to me it's a bad day at a theme park."

Or fast-food institutions: "McDonald's is hiring senior citizens. This must be part of their cradle-to-grave minimum-wage program. It's nice to know that when you're eighty you can make the exact same money you made when you were sixteen."

To Leno, certain topics aren't funny and he maintains a lot of people agree with him about that.

"More and more people are telling me how much they dislike the mean-spirited material—the ethnic bashing, women bashing, gay bashing—that was big for a while on TV. There will always be a place for dirty *in* comedy. When it's done right, funny is funny. No one is ever bothered by George Carlin's material. He's never mean-spirited."

Leno, however, has nothing good to say about Andrew Dice Clay, whose bad-guy image is the antithesis of Leno's. Leno asked *TV Guide* in 1991, "Have you seen Andrew Dice Clay anywhere lately? That concert film of his that Twentieth

Century-Fox has decided not to release—it probably wasn't because of its dirt, but because it had no real jokes in it."

Leno doesn't use props in his comic routines, though on and off he did a recurrent bit with funny products when he was guest-hosting the "Tonight Show."

"I used to feel guilty when I walked onstage in Vegas and didn't have lights and lasers," Leno said, "but then people would come up and say how much they enjoyed just being talked to. People are so used to being lip-synched and teched out that they think it's amazing that people can do things by themselves. I think you need that communication. That's why I like comedy—it's real low-tech."

For this reason he won't make videos or records or tapes. "We live in a society where people rent a movie and watch it by themselves on a thirteen-inch screen and then they say, 'I didn't think that was very funny.' It's the difference between standing outside a club and listening to the jokes or coming inside and laughing with the other people."

Leno's wife, Mavis, once summed up Leno's image of himself:

"Jay is a man with an almost limitless amount of goodwill. That comes across onstage no matter what he's saying. Jay sees himself as just a regular guy."

6

Heeere's Jay

Leno won't tell dirty jokes, so he says, but he will tell condom jokes. And he will tell Geraldo jokes. He lumps them together as, collectively, "condom-Geraldo" jokes.

In short, a condom-Geraldo joke is a surefire joke that is just a tad, well, racy. It is a joke constructed to make sure that the studio audience in greater Burbank responds positively and explosively to the monologue—just in case the Sununu joke or the Dan Quayle joke or the President Bush joke has sailed over the audience's head earlier.

He once told *Washington Post* critic Tom Shales: "If there *is* a condom-Geraldo joke, it's usually the last one."

Leno doesn't *mind* dirty jokes. He doesn't believe there's anything *wrong* with blue material, as long as it's funny. In his early years he did looser stuff, but he feels he is too old now to tell sex jokes without looking like a jerk. He cited what he calls his "thirty-nine-and-a-half rule" about blue material to Jennifer Tucker of the *Tampa Tribune:*

When a woman sees a guy twenty-seven or twenty-eight with a full head of hair do a dirty joke on the stage, she thinks that's cute and sexy. "Oh, I can't *believe* he said that! Hee, hee!" But when a woman sees a guy thirty-nine and a half, with his guts hanging out over his belt and a bald spot gleaming where his hair should be, then it's more likely, "Oooooh! That *old* guy. He's really *gross!*"

The older Leno gets, the more he molds his act to fit his style of delivery so he can live with it at ease. Clean comedy is just something he's comfortable with.

"I find it more interesting and more challenging to try to write something that's clean and funny and appeals to everybody."

That must be why *Vanity Fair* called him "the Mr. Clean of contemporary comedy." He himself likes blue humor when the right comedian is doing it. But he believes in never taking a "cheap shot" at anybody or anything. That's where the "Mr. Clean" idea comes from. His repartee never crosses the boundary between wry and offensive.

"Comedy is supposed to be the underdog making fun of the big guy," he says. "I get annoyed when I see humor that is fascist or racist. Or misogynist or anti-Semitic. I defend people's right to say whatever they want. I just don't particularly care for it.

"I wouldn't mind if there was a *joke* there. It's always funny to me how if you make fun of ethnic groups or make fun of women or something like that, then you're on the cutting edge, but if you go after our foreign policy or the savings-and-loan scandal or Washington, that's just like getting a Walt Disney G rating."

In the midst of comics like Andrew Dice Clay and the late Sam Kinison, he has become something of a hero for the nice-folk masses.

"I think I've become popular by default," he said. "Standards have dropped so low that I look good by comparison."

"It's like giving you a prize for *not* walking down the street and robbing someone. Being well-known is okay, but everyone just assumes you must be a wimp or a jerk if you're a comic."

Taking a look at his attitude on comedy and analyzing it, he said:

"My job is to kind of degrade and humiliate the whole system fairly equally." The topics he still hews to whenever he can—the jokes that get the laughs—are the ones that have always gotten laughs: sex, money, and alcohol.

"Those things will always get laughs because that's something everybody knows. Everybody's had brushes with sex, money, and alcohol."

And yet, when you move over into obscenity, or the far reaches of the subject of sex, you reach a point of no return. Obscenity is *boring,* Leno told Lawrence Christon of the *Los Angeles Times.* "People yell at you in traffic and give you the finger. You're running up against it all day long. You don't need to pay twenty dollars to hear a guy swear at you from the stage.

"Oh, a few people are successful with it, like Richard Pryor. But it's a moral thing. You see a grandfather and a little kid, you don't want to yell obscene words at them. I don't object to it in other comedians. I just don't do it."

One of the strongest jokes we will hear from Leno is the one about Gary Hart:

"I was on a plane the other day and Gary Hart sat across the aisle. And it was so strange: here's a man who almost got to be president of the United States, and my wife walks by him and says to me, 'Oh, I hope he doesn't grab my ass.'"

Leno especially enjoys taking potshots at hypocrites. "Americans do have a good sense of fair play. And hypocrisy is the best for comedians. People can get away with anything, except just don't be a hypocrite about it. That's the number one thing."

He uses a rapid-fire delivery when performing his monologue on the "Tonight Show." He knows that the audience at home will turn the channel if he doesn't catch their attention with a fast-and-furious onslaught of gags.

Unlike Carson, Leno doesn't "die" well; that is, he cannot turn a joke that misfires into a laugh. Nobody did that better than Carson; oftentimes he was at his funniest when he was dying onstage.

Some critics maintain that when Leno does his monologue he seems out of it because he shows little reaction to the audience. If a joke bombs, he goes right on into the next joke, usually laughing to himself. If the joke goes over well with the audience, he has the same chuckling response.

At the time he was guest-hosting the "Tonight Show," he once explained his modus operandi for creating monologues. A typical late-night talk-show stand-up runs about seven or eight minutes in length. Leno likes to think of the monologue as a kind of dramatic "day in brief"—structured in a manner similar to the sequence of a newspaper.

"You open with a few jokes about whatever the big story of the day is," he told Dale.Anderson of the *Buffalo News*. "And then, as you move through it, you get to the lesser stories. Then maybe there are a couple of jokes about social issues—you know, like 'Dear Abby'—or a sports joke. Then near the end of the monologue, you tend to do more jokes about entertainment, about commercials, or about television shows."

The opener usually is *the* big story of the day, but not *always*, especially if a headlining story is so tragic that you cannot be funny about it. If so, the rule is to use a substitute story, but at least something *new*.

After the lead story comes the next-biggest story, or joke, and so on, running through a group of related and/or unrelated jokes to the final olio of columns and features that wind up the routine.

The dynamics of the stand-up is always the same: a smash opening; a group of quick jabs to the funny bone; some smaller ones; a number of scatter shots; and a big one to end on.

In actually creating the routine, Leno would start out putting together his one-night-a-week routine on the morning of the day *before* he was going to deliver it. By the time he started, he would have mentally gathered together a number of new jokes. These he would arrange in a kind of logical sequence, paying attention to the dynamics of the routine itself.

By the end of the day, he would have about fifty to sixty gags ready to work on. This preliminary work was all cerebral. Now came the nitty-gritty. The litmus test, as it were.

For the litmus test, Leno would assemble a clutch of his favorite comedic friends at the house for a final appraisal of the material. It was the habit of good friends to drop by the house on comedy night to join in on the fun. The food was fast, the drinks minimal, the dialogue slick. Munching hamburgers, fried chicken, pizza—or any kind of fast-food available and tasty—the group of comedians would sit around until the wee small hours of the morning, honing the jokes down to a select sharp twenty-five.

He points out that he usually always goes with what's in the news. But he never wants to get *ahead* of the audience, as he did on one occasion recently with a joke about John Poindexter.

The joke: "Recording star James Brown served only six months of his six-year sentence, and now I understand John Poindexter is taking singing and dancing lessons."

When he finished the joke he waited for the laugh. Didn't *everybody* know that James Brown was a famous singer? Didn't *everybody* know that John Poindexter was in trouble?

Maybe not.

There was no response. There was, in fact, not even a murmur of any kind. No reaction at all. Obviously, no one knew who John Poindexter was nor had any idea what Leno was talking about. In fact, it might have been a double-barreled misfire. They might not even have known who James

Brown was. Leno was dying onstage, and there was nothing he could do about it. He simply went on to the next joke and tried to get back up to speed.

It's a big problem for a comic: to find subjects that people know about, and also subjects where the *good* guys and the *bad* guys are evident. The Poindexter-Brown fiasco points up the reason Leno—and other stand-up comics—will choose certain surefire subjects rather than opt for subjects that are obscure.

There's always inept politicos. There's always dumb TV shows. There's always recognized nonentities such as the country's vice president, whoever he is. It's the *job* that's the joke, as about as important, John Nance Garner once said, as a "pitcher of warm spit."

Leno's version: "Some people think that April Fools' Day is kind of silly. Taking one day out of the year to honor the vice president—I don't think that's too much."

And of course, there is McDonald's. The perfect target. That's something *everyone* knows. Leno never knocks the food—just the way the stuff is served, along with the kids who serve it.

Finally, when all else fails, he does a condom-Geraldo joke. The surefire blue joke. Examples:

One: "I hear there's talk of inaugurating a National Condom Week. Now *there's* a parade you don't want to miss."

Two: "In New York City they're handing out condoms to high school students. Gee, I thought it was a big day when I got my class ring."

Three: A swipe at Geraldo Rivera's cavalier advertisements for himself and his talk show: "I'll tell you something. I lost all respect for Charles Manson when he went on that show."

Four: "*Consumer Reports*. This month was their condom-testing issue. Spent the whole month testing condoms. Boy, I bet these guys couldn't *wait* to get to work in the morning."

Pause. Pretense of greeting a companion: "Johnson! You're two hours early for work—*again!*"

To be a successful comedian, Leno says, "You really have to put yourself in the place of the people in the audience. If I see someone who's not laughing, my instinct isn't to get annoyed—it's to figure out why they don't understand. Sometimes it's not that someone's dumb, it's just that they're not educated.

"Now, with colleges today, you have the brightest crowds, but they're very naive. They don't know much about life. You can't talk about sex, really, other than the thrill of it. So you can't share any of your life experiences."

Different audiences laugh at different things, Leno went on. "But say, whenever I have a large Oriental audience, I tell them, 'I was watching "Bonanza," you know, Hop Sing [the Cartwrights' Chinese manservant]. . . . Why is it whenever a person of Asian descent enters, the producer feels the need to do that stupid melody: *ling-ding?* They don't do this for white people: when Clint Eastwood comes on, they don't play "How Much Is That Doggie in the Window?" When I do that, Oriental people come up after the show and say, "Oh, you know, my father, he gets mad when they do that on TV!"'

In white heat Leno lambasted the current political humor, which he finds racist. "Or like what passes for political humor now. These morning deejays, they say these racist things. I was in Dallas—it was Martin Luther King's birthday—and some deejay said something about, 'If they shot two more, we'd get the whole week off.' And this was considered outrageous—it's not. It's just *racist.*

"It's the same thing with the way they treat women. In fact, the only shows I really don't like are all-men shows. When they expect you to be really stupid or vulgar, I just don't do that kind of stuff. My mom was a big influence. I genuinely like women. You watch comedians now: marriage always stinks, no one ever makes love after marriage. Just by being reasonably egalitarian, I get more women who come up and thank me for not doing bimbo jokes or 'my wife' jokes. It's so stupid!"

Though he derides politicians he is much like them in that he wants everybody to be his friend. The only difference is that a politician wants as many votes as possible, whereas Leno wants as many laughs as possible.

He allows that he is afraid of making jokes about sponsors. After all, these people pay his salary on the "Tonight Show."

"It's a funny thing," Leno said. "You can make fun of presidents and vice presidents but not sponsors. I mean it. I think the audience perceives advertising and corporations to be more powerful than the president or vice president."

One night, after the *Exxon Valdez* oil spill in Alaska, Leno told the "Tonight Show" audience a joke about the captain of the *Valdez*. Leno compared him to Otis, the drunk on the old "Andy Griffith Show." It got a big laugh.

Leno explained to Mary Billard at *Gentlemen's Quarterly* exactly how he had worked up the *Valdez*-Otis joke. First, the image of Otis tickled Leno's fancy, and that was the kernel of the idea. "Right away, Otis conjures up an image of a heavy-set guy who hasn't shaved."

Then Leno decided *not* to make the obvious play for the pun—"half-baked Alaska."

The second part of building the joke was in trying to figure out somewhere you could take a boat, into some kind of small inlet—but Leno was unable to come up with any reasonable place.

"I tried the Strait of Hormuz," Leno said, "but that didn't sound good. I tried the Cape of Good Hope. There aren't many people who know those are the worst waters in the world, you know, trying to get around the Cape."

He threw in the towel when he couldn't think of an

appropriate waterway and decided to edit the joke down. He was left with just the simple idea of a drunk making huge, weaving, ten-mile turns, in unfriendly waters.

When he did the joke, he pantomimed the spiflicated Otis trying to steer a lurching boat through heavy waters: "Oh, look out, look out—*wow!*"

Leno considers certain words funny by themselves— words such as *Harvey Wallbanger, discos,* and *Donna Summer.* He calls these "punch words." "People just react to them with a laugh."

Sometimes he deliberately inserts bad jokes into his monologue, knowing that they will bomb, so he can play to the negative response of his audience. For example, referring again to the *Valdez* spill, he used this one:

"Exxon's got a new promotion going now." Pause. "With every fill-up, you get a set of drinking glasses depicting all the wildlife they've killed."

Leno commented: "It's a real hard joke. You are conjuring up an image that people don't want to hear. Oh, gee! You think of the ducks and the otters—just dying—and oh, it's not a comfortable thing for people to think of."

Anticipating that the joke would bomb, Leno prepared an amusing response to the audience's possible groan. "So when they go, 'Ooohhh,' then I can scream and go, 'Oh! It's my fault. . . . Yell at me!'"

The night he did the *Valdez* routine he still had doubts that it would get any laughs. "That night I kept saying to myself, Jesus, is this Exxon stuff going to be too harsh? Well, I realize now it wasn't. In fact, the next week I was able to step it up a little and see what the mood of the country was then."

He retools his jokes to fit the audience he is facing as well as the time frame of the event that he happens to be talking about.

"When you're doing a college, you can talk about the neo-Nazi fascists at the phone company, and when you do a Perry Como show, you'd say, 'Those crazy people at the phone company are unbelievable.'"

Once he reworked a doubtful joke by rejiggering nothing but the lead-in. From the start, the opening phrase had never seemed to work.

"I had this joke about going to Europe and walking into the Vatican gift shop, where I found the same crummy stuff you see everywhere—you know, the 'Where's the beef?' T-shirts, and so forth.

"But I found that if I said that I went to Europe, I got something negative from the crowd. Because, of course, most of them do not go to Europe. It was as though I had distanced myself from them.

"People said to me, 'Go on; do the joke anyway.' I said, 'No, I can feel it. It's like they think I'm trying to show off. Like I'm name-dropping or something.'"

In 1984, when Leno went to Europe, he took his parents along. And the very fact that he had done that gave him the right opener for the joke.

He began it by saying, "Hey, I bought my ticket to heaven; I took my parents to Europe." And suddenly the joke that followed was okay.

When the audience heard that he had given his parents a nice present, the reaction was favorable. "Oh, isn't that nice," they seemed to say.

Leno maintains that comedians must be like everyone else. They have to be like the people who make up the audience. He told a struggling comedian who did jokes about his first cocaine experience, "You know, most people don't do cocaine. I don't do cocaine." Then he explained, "When you're a comedian, you have to be similar enough to share experiences."

In the art of joke making, Leno believes that a well-constructed joke is not necessarily the funniest joke possible. "It's just well constructed. It's believable. It makes sense."

Leno thinks of comedy as "instinctual." "I have no interest in *thinking* about it. I have no books about comedy. Walk around my house, you'd have a hard time figuring out what I do for a living. You'd probably think I was a mechanic because I have so many car books. I don't have masks of comedy and tragedy, or Ed Wynn's hat on a hook. When you start *thinking* about comedy, you become a humorist or a satirist, and eventually you're out of business."

Comedy doesn't change throughout the ages, Leno told *Los Angeles Magazine.* "Comedy's pretty constant. It never really changes. The same things that are funny now have always been funny. If you watch the Keystone Kops or Keaton or Chaplin, you'll see they hold up very well because nothing has changed. I don't think any differently than Alan King did. I don't take his jokes, but I use the same mock outrage, the same annoyance at things. Good comedy isn't doing things differently, it's doing the same things better."

Leno insists the audience must know what you are talking about before it will laugh. Maybe this is the reason Letterman has a smaller audience than Leno. Sometimes Letterman's jokes are so hip only he and a few others know what he's talking about.

In any case, Leno once gave an example of a joke that was accessible to the audience and, as a result, drew gales of laughter from them.

The joke went, "Nancy Reagan's idea of the Third World is JCPenney." That got "a real laugh," according to Leno. "It is something people understand. They know the first part, so they understand the second part."

To analyze a joke and show why it got laughs, Leno selected the following:

"President Reagan has now come out against the electric

chair." Pause. "He feels there are now so many men on death row, he would like to have electric bleachers." Leno called this a "simple joke," yet he resolved it into many components, showing that its structure is much more complex than it appears on the surface.

Here is Leno's breakdown of the joke:

Have you heard this? President Reagan has now come out against the electric chair.

Leno: "People will listen because they know that's contrary to what he believes—or at least what he is thought to believe. 'Oooh!' says the audience."

He feels there are now so many men on death row . . .

Leno: "This is a thoroughly logical reason to back up the president's purported change of mind."

. . . he would like to have electric bleachers.

Leno: "Instead of just an electric chair, the president opts for many chairs—'bleachers.' The fact that the word *bleachers* usually refers to an audience and not the victim of the chair makes no difference. The word *bleachers* immediately reaffirms what the audience already thinks about Reagan."

Leno does not like preachy jokes. He does not like the would-be comic who strolls on the talk-show set and turns into a pompous and stuffy bore. The place for the preacher, Leno believes, is in the pulpit, not behind the microphone. There is nothing duller that a comic playing philosopher. Unless it's a philosopher playing comic.

That's the reason Leno loved the "Letterman" show, even though his approach to humor there was different from his approach on the "Tonight Show."

A "Letterman" appearance, he says, requires a very dissimilar type of preparation from a "Tonight Show" guest-host gig.

First of all, when Leno did the "Letterman" monologue, he was required to get quick laughs. It was an obligation, a part of the territory, what he was paid to do. Then, when he finally sat down, he had an even tougher proposition: he had to keep David Letterman on the edge of laughter, or he'd have Letterman telling him he was an infantile idiot.

And that brings one to the stories. Leno could tell David Letterman amusing little stories—about his experiences, about his parents, about his travels, about anything. But Letterman knew how to handle comics. He refused to carry them.

"Refusing to carry them" meant that if Leno leaned onto the old familiar comic's crutch—"Dave, did you ever see *Gone With the Wind?*"—Letterman would invariably respond, "No. I have never heard of it. What is it?" He would deny he knew something about *anything*.

"Dave, have you ever seen the Empire State Building?"

"No. I've never seen the Empire State Building. I've never heard of it. Has it been built yet?"

That's part of Letterman's pixie humor. And it made the routine itself even funnier.

But it took Leno a lot of preparation to line up his stories, and it took perspiration as well as inspiration to get them to work.

"Dave's show has been great for me," Leno told Mark Faris at the *Akron Beacon Journal.* "The format is more oriented to my age group and humor. It's not like some of those shows where they fry an egg and talk about cellulite.

"It's given me more of a chance to do the kind of humor I like—which is not always possible when you're opening for someone, you have to tailor your material in order to suit an audience that comes to see, say, Perry Como, or somebody like that who would draw an older crowd."

George Carlin, Robert Klein, and Freddie Prinze were big influences on Leno's comedy, but there were certainly others in the past whom he studied in building his own type of humor.

Leno was recently reminiscing about the old days when

his type of comedy was just coming in vogue. "It all started with Freddie Prinze," he said. "Freddie and I used to be roommates. Then Freddie hit, and all of a sudden there was this idea of twenty-year-old people being comedians. Every high school and college kid in the country suddenly wanted to do this. The clubs were filled. Every class clown that ever lived started showing up in the clubs."

Leno and Prinze were close friends in those days. Leno would stay at Prinze's apartment when he was working in New York. When Prinze was playing Boston, Leno would return the favor. In fact, it was Leno who taught Prinze how to drive.

"People are always saying Freddie killed himself because he was successful," Leno observed. "But they didn't know Freddie. I knew another comedian who killed himself because he *never* made it. Success wasn't Freddie's problem." Leno turned thoughtful, then changed the subject.

"It probably started *really* with Robert Klein and George Carlin and all those guys in the late sixties. Before 1969, most comedians were white, middle-aged men talking about, 'Oh, my wife, I can't believe it. . . .' I would laugh at these guys more through my father's eyes than through my own.

"Before that, comedians were for everybody. Milton Berle. Everybody laughed at him. All of a sudden, in 1969, you had comedians for people over forty and under forty. That was the cutoff point. There were the young guys who made fun of the old guys and the old guys who thought the new guys were insolent punks. It was a changing around."

As for the older comedians who acted as models for him, Leno remembered one in particular. "I used to like Alan King because he would come out and rail at the phone companies and the airlines. You never knew how much of it was con-trived, but he generally had an anger that I thought was funny."

And there was Bob Newhart, too. And of course, Mort

Sahl—in spite of the fact that Leno did not model himself on Sahl at all.

"He did it with such a sharp wit that even people who didn't want to hear what he said admitted, 'Yeah, Sahl's right.' I like people who work within certain confines and can be clever within those confines. Guys who don't do shtick, such as Bob Newhart or Robert Klein—that's the kind of stuff I want to do."

As to his favorite subject, Leno has a ready answer. "One of my favorite subjects in comedy is injustice, but I think rebellion is funniest when it comes from within the system. Comedy is essentially conservative. You need to come from a conservative background. Take someone like Sam Kinison. For his stuff on marriage to be funny, he had to set it up in a conservative way, like: 'I was married. We had a little house. We had an idyllic thing.' He'd set it up that way, and then go into a rant."

Leno is wary of using controversial jokes, even though he has revised his opinion on controversy since landing the "Tonight Show" job.

But he usually prefers to denigrate an evil that is a politically correct evil—such as drugs. He wants to steer clear of any evil that might be in some gray, undecided, or indefinable area.

For example:

"A lot of people in Colombia feel that Americans have no right to go down there and interfere." Leno meant, interfere in politics, of course, to stop the drug trade. "But Americans think, 'Sure we do [have a right to interfere], because in America, the customer is always right.'"

And of course, it's always politically correct for Leno to assail himself. He likes to puncture the balloon of his own fame. Here's one shortie:

"I got a two-page spread in *Newsweek*. I called my buddies back home." Pause. "They don't get *Newsweek*."

Leno believes in the equality of the sexes and frequently sounds off about the injustice of some macho quirks in Western society.

"I always wondered who wrote the notes for the movies in *TV Guide*. And I realized it must be a man. It couldn't be woman." Pause. "I saw a listing: 'Nine o'clock—HBO movie. *Unmarried Woman*, the story of a divorced woman's struggle for respect and equality. Starring Alan Bates.'"

Going out of his way not to offend women, he never does wife jokes.

"I mean, when you listen to comedy now, all marriages suck. Any woman you've been with more than a week is a bitch usually or bad sexually or something." To duck controversy he will not do jokes about politicians' views on abortion or women's rights. He added a qualifying statement, however: "Well, maybe if the joke is real funny."

Leno doesn't use comedy to change the world because he's "not a social satirist. If it's funny, fine."

When he first used to try out his weekly monologue at a comedy club before going on the "Tonight Show" with it, he spoke with a deliberately uninflected voice to the audience to see whether or not the joke was good enough to work on its own.

"I can always jazz up a joke with body English to get a laugh, but first I need to know if it works by itself."

On the "Tonight Show" he'll throw in "yeah, yeah"'s if the audience doesn't laugh. His trademark "yeah, yeah"'s and "hey"'s help induce laughter when all else—the joke—fails.

He doesn't like deleting jokes he has lined up for the "Tonight Show" as Carson was wont to do. In order to edit out jokes while he was onstage before the audience, Carson had his cue cards spread out from left to right in front of him. If he thought a joke wouldn't go over with the crowd that night, he would simply skip it.

Leno, however, employs a single cue-card boy to hold a pile of the cards, revealing them one at a time, thus making it impossible for him to jump from one joke to another at will. He has to work his way from the first joke to the second, etc. Each joke leads into the next, making it impossible for him to edit any out.

Leno explained his rationale for this modus operandi in this fashion:

"I do them this way because then I have to do the joke. That's just my own personal thing. If the monologue isn't doing well, I can't bail. Because I have to do this joke to get to that joke. You go out there and you do the joke. And I figure if I'm going to stay up all night putting these jokes together, I should at least do them."

Leno tries to keep his personal leanings out of his political jokes. He takes shots at all politicians—Republicans and Democrats, liberals and conservatives.

Leno has bragged, "I don't think anybody can figure out my politics. I'm not someone who hopefully ever will have his picture taken with a politician. If you get invited to the White House or something, that's different, that's a presidential thing. But if you're out there shaking hands with a candidate, or you're out there at a fund-raiser, you can't then go on the 'Tonight Show' and make fun of the opposing candidate."

Jerry Seinfeld once described Leno's philosophy of comedy this way:

"One great Leno line is, 'Props—the enemy of wit.' And whenever we're watching someone do a shot on Carson or Letterman, he's always snapping his fingers and going, *'Jokes! Jokes! Jokes!'*

"Because that's his philosophy. You've got to have a steady rhythm of jokes that you can snap your fingers to. It's not so much that you understand the lyrics, but it's got to be good to dance to. Ultimately he wants everyone to do exactly as he does—only less well."

Perhaps the main goal of Leno's comedic approach is to point out absurdity to the middle class, the kind of absurdity an ordinary guy can encounter in his life. Or an ordinary gal in her life. This he accomplishes better than any other current comedian.

One way he reaches his goal is through the architecture of his material. How a joke is constructed is important to Leno. He can spend days rewriting a one-liner.

"You've really got to structure jokes the way you would a book or a sentence. If I said *car* two jokes ago, I'll say *automobile* this time around, or *vehicle*—just to keep that meter. It has to be interesting sounding, as well as being funny. I really go over each word, and I say, 'There's one too many words in this sentence. What can I take out? What can I add?' Because the trick is to get to the joke as quickly as possible. That's the whole thing in comedy.

"You try to work with a formula. For example, they've got this stupid TV show called 'Finder of Lost Loves.' Now I've got a couple different ways to approach it. I was going to approach it from the way of, 'You know, it's amazing. Here we are in this country, and we can't get the FBI to set up a hot line for runaway children, but we have a police force to find a girl I used to go out with.'

"I may either do it that way or from the standpoint of, 'Gee—that girl that threw up in my car. I wonder what happened to her. I'd like to find her.'

"I'll try it a number of ways before I see which one works best. I'll spend the next three or four days putting that line together."

When he was on a gig in Atlantic City and working out a joke for a later "Tonight" guest-host appearance, Leno discussed the evolution of a joke with Graydon Carter, a *Rolling Stone* writer.

Checking one of his index cards with the joke written on it, Leno said, "I'm trying to decide. A couple—where is it? Tennessee. A couple in Tennessee are getting divorced and are arguing about their frozen embryos. And I say, 'You know what's bad? How about the kids? It's hard enough to accept the fact that you're adopted. But now you're defrosted. You're adopted *and* defrosted.'"

Later on, he shortened the routine to the original punch line and added another one while in his dressing room.

"It's tough enough finding out you're adopted. Now you find out you're defrosted. A Tennessee couple are divorcing and they're arguing over who gets the frozen embryos. And you thought dividing up the record albums would be tough."

The joke later appeared in its final form on the "Tonight Show." There, Leno said:

"This is kind of sad. Have you heard about this couple in New Jersey that are getting a divorce and they're fighting over custody of their frozen embryos? See, I feel sorry for the frozen embryos. You know, it's tough enough when you're a kid growing up and later finding out you're adopted, but to find out you've been *defrosted* . . . !

Only by extensive rewriting had he been able to get the joke down pat. In short, writing a joke is not as easy as it might appear to be. You have to work hard at it. And nobody works harder at it or with more determination than Jay Leno.

7

Captain of the Comedy Ship

L ENO WORKS SO HARD at his job that he has become a kind of comedy commander, a banana of all bananas, to put it another way.

Indeed it was his commanding presence that was the reason his wife, Mavis, was attracted to him when she first laid eyes on him at the Comedy Store in 1976. As she once put it, Leno seemed to be captain of the comedy ship.

Kevin Rooney agrees with Mavis that Leno is the leader whenever the comedians congregate. According to Rooney, Leno gives "sermons on the mount" to his fellow comedians whenever they are at his home in Beverly Hills. Rooney says that Leno gets a big kick out of these get-togethers.

"It's usually midnight or one o'clock, and Mavis has gone to sleep," Rooney went on. "He will sit on his couch and we'll all be on the other couches—Larry Miller, Jerry Seinfeld, Dennis Miller, myself. You have to watch the 'Tonight Show' and 'Letterman.' Those are your schools, sort of technique things.

"Then Leno will fly around the cable dial, all one hundred stations, at a blinding speed. It's a psychotic experience. Just as you start to look at something, he's moved on to something else. If there's not a joke there or something interesting to make fun of, it's gone. *Click!*"

Another Leno friend, Jerry Seinfeld, claims that Leno will not admit he is successful, even though Seinfeld feels Leno is at the top of the heap of professional comedians. This observation jibes, of course, with Leno's regular-guy image.

Seinfeld has explained this aspect of Leno's character as follows:

"You have to realize that success is the great poison of stand-up comedy because it takes away the hunger and it takes away the fight you need to make your shows good every night."

Without that hunger, a comedian simply strolls out in a leisurely fashion and tends to do the same old thing he's always done. He feels no *need* to prove himself to a new audience. When there is no need to prove himself, the comedian has sundered all the underpinnings of proper motivation.

Seinfeld is familiar enough with Leno to know that he *must* feel he has not yet achieved success in order to get people to laugh. If every aspect of his life shows him that he has succeeded, he must never face the fact or admit it. He must *ignore* success.

To Leno, the term *comedy star* is an oxymoron. If one is in comedy and becomes a star, he is no longer a comedian. Likewise, if a star should become a comedian, then he is no longer a star.

"A comedian," Seinfeld concludes, echoing Leno, "has got to be somebody I *do* know and I can relate to."

Leno is a workaholic. He will even do his routines when he is sick. In 1989 he appeared onstage with a terrible cold.

"It all disappears," he said. "I have a cold now. I've been sick for a couple of days. But really, people who work for a living don't want to hear about this. Because I don't want to hear some whiny show-business performer going, 'Oh, and then I got there and *of course the limo was blue instead of black.*'"

One time Leno even took the stage with a broken rib digging into his chest after a motorbike fall. The pain didn't faze him a bit.

"I was onstage for like forty-five minutes, and boy, it was fine. I mean, I was aware of it, but gosh, it was fine. And then when I got off, *'Whoooof!* Ow! What did I do?'"

Leno is so determined to win over his audience he will fix his eyes on the most intelligent-looking and aloof person there until that poor soul comes to wish he had never set foot in the auditorium. This person is Leno's primary challenge. If he can win over this sourpuss, he considers his comedy routine a success. Therefore, unlike most performers, Leno prefers working with the houselights on so he can eyeball the crowd.

Leno is big on body language. During routines he whacks the palm of one hand with the back of the other. He slices his hand through his hair. Even at "rest" he keeps a foot always tapping. *Time*'s Richard Stengel called him "a perpetual-motion machine."

He tries to ridicule *every* politician so as not to show favoritism or hew to any particular party line. For instance, he would joke about presidential candidate Paul Tsongas —a Democrat—as well as Vice President Quayle—a Republican.

Vis-à-vis Tsongas, Leno said, "Let's see, he's a liberal, he's from Massachusetts, he's got a Greek name. Say, that sounds like a winning combination!"

Or what about the classic Teddy Kennedy joke: "If no other contenders emerge, Kennedy could have the nomination in his pocket. Now if he could just find his pants, that would be great."

According to Leno, that specific Kennedy joke "gets a huge laugh. So much bigger than the joke really warrants."

Jerry Brown, aka Governor Moonbeam of California, also received his share of comic abuse from Leno.

"Jerry Brown's been working pretty good. The sad thing

about the Brown candidacy is that all the people who want to vote for him are locked inside that Biosphere II experiment."

Sometimes a political joke can cause trouble for Leno, and then he'll delete it from his routines. Once he told a joke about Rep. William Gray's decision to leave the House of Representatives to become head of the United Negro College Fund:

"I said I can understand why he quit Congress. A mind is a terrible thing to waste." It was a funny joke, holding up Congress as a laughingstock, but Leno was told by people that it might be construed as racist. As a result, he consigned the joke to comedy limbo.

Leno had decided that the audience might think he was making fun of the slogan "A mind is a terrible thing to waste," when in reality it was *Congress* he was making the butt of his gibe.

"What happens is people only hear what they want to hear. They hear you doing the slogan and they think you're making fun of the slogan. So I haven't done the joke anymore."

Leno is obviously a man who knows what he is about when it comes to analyzing jokes and audience reaction to them.

He won't tell jokes about junk-bond king Mike Milken on account of Milken's out-and-out loathsomeness. Leno finds him repulsive even when compared to the likes of rich, self-centered yuppie prototype Donald Trump.

"At least Trump employs people; at least he builds something." Milken even loses out to no less an international monster than Qaddafi. "Qaddafi's a madman, but at least he built hospitals." Leno still isn't through with Milken. "Even Bolivian drug dealers give something back to the community."

Leno has been accused of being a "technician" as

opposed to a "conceptual" comedian. Leno once told *Philadelphia* magazine: "I don't mind if someone says I'm a technician. If they say nobody laughs, *then* I want to know why. The idea is to pack as many jokes into an area as you can. You try to do what people like, and not what you like."

Leno smiled. "There's an old saying. When the band laughs, you're out of show business."

He studies other comedians carefully, profiting from their strikeouts as well as their home runs.

"I see comedians doing incredibly hip material that only the other comedians laugh at. The audience has no idea what the comic is talking about. If I get into a situation where it's a rough crowd and the people aren't paying attention, I'll turn into a technician and bark out jokes as fast as I can just to get the roll going."

He thought a moment. "But if it's late at night, and the crowd is kind of hip, then I can get conceptual."

It's all a matter of reading the crowd—making sure that the audience sees things the same way *he* sees things.

That's the reason Leno made it a practice to try out his guest-hosting "Tonight Show" material at mainstream comedy clubs like the Comedy and Magic Club in Hermosa Beach before doing his once-a-week guest-host routine on the "Tonight Show." After all, the TV audience of the "Tonight Show" is mainstream middle America, unlike the audiences of the Improv, which is frequented by jaded members of the comedy profession.

Leno has come a long way from the Nixon-what-a-jerk comedy clubs in Greenwich Village. Instead of slamming Nixon, Leno will now pick out other public figures, such as Saddam Hussein these days—"I must say the first time I saw him I said, 'Oh, look, Noriega's face cleared up.'"

Nancy Reagan is fair game for Leno's jokes, too. When her book *My Turn* came out, he claimed it was made into the movie bomb *She-Devil.*

But that was a mild one compared to this.

"I read that Nancy Reagan was at the Beverly Hills Hotel to accept her Humanitarian of the Year Award. I'm glad she beat out that conniving bitch Mother Teresa."

Leno even does Prescott Bush jokes nowadays. "Here's one I was going to try about Prescott Bush. You know, the president's brother. You're aware they say he's involved with the Japanese Mafia. He says he didn't know why, but he woke up one morning and found the front end of a Toyota in his bed."

Once in a while Leno does jokes about ordinary people, focusing on such targets as the security guards at the "Tonight Show" soundstage:

"Security guys are the ones who know least about what's going on. At NBC there was a guy who stopped me and said, 'Who're you?'

"'Jay Leno,' I said. 'I'm hosting the "Tonight Show."'

"'Right,' the guy says. 'Johnny Carson hosts the "Tonight Show."'

"'I'm subbing for him.'

"'Right. So what's your name?' The guy picks up the phone and says, 'I have a Jim Reynolds here who says he's hosting the "Tonight Show."'

"'It's not Jim Reynolds. It's Jay Leno. Jay!' Jeez." Leno. Pronounced Lenn-oh, not Lee-noh.

Leno prefers ridiculing famous people because they're in the news and audiences know whom he's talking about. Like the one about acting:

"Stallone and Schwarzenegger have opened up the acting profession to a lot of people who couldn't get into it when speech was a major requirement."

Or the one about Liberace.

"I've got to show you this old magazine I just bought." [Pause.] "It's got an article by Liberace called 'What I Want in a Woman.'"

Or the one about Lee Iacocca.

"Lee Iacocca has turned down the Pennsylvania governor's invitation to fill a vacant seat in the U.S. Senate. I think he did the right thing. Do we really need a senator whose slogan is: 'If you can find a better politician, buy him'?"

Of course if the audience doesn't know that Iacocca is the chairman of Chrysler, whose slogan is "If you can find a better car, buy it," they won't laugh. Leno's jokes work because he's usually exactly on the same wave length as the audience is.

Sometimes his best intentions backfire. There was one incident with Roseanne Barr.

After he had made fun of her in one of his routines, he ran into her at the Improv. She immediately upbraided him. She told him she was upset because he was always kidding her about her weight.

Leno was surprised as well as puzzled. He reminded her that on a recent HBO special she had made a remark to the effect that "we fat people have to stick together."

She said that was beside the point. She didn't want to hear about the fact that she was overweight anymore. Leno felt that if she didn't want to be teased that way, he wouldn't do any more fat jokes about her.

And he never did.

He likes to joke about fast food and certain other products, such as Yugos. For Yugo cars, Leno has said, "A new antitheft device is to make the name larger." On the Letterman show Leno once cracked, "And Yugo had trouble passing the 1993 crash test. You know, they couldn't get the dummy to go in the car."

McDonald's is not safe from Leno's barbs either. "McDonald's has the McRib sandwich—they're determined to use every part of that cow. What's next? The McCowhead?"

He'll always go after a cheap airline.

"It was like stepping into the hold of some kind of flying slave ship. The flight attendant was Helga the stomping mare, wearing a Mayan death mask."

Or just airlines in general.

"They say you're safer in the air than you are in your own bathroom. But I never slipped on the toilet and fell thirty-five thousand feet. I never moved the shower curtain and had a fireball come out and incinerate me."

And what about airline food?

"The stewardess said, 'You can have either the sirloin steak or tapioca chicken.' I never heard of tapioca chicken!"

Another time he told an audience about an article that said most airplane injuries occur on the ground. Looking shocked, he said, "Of course, it's not until you hit the ground that you experience that minor discomfort."

Leno likes cerebral jokes. "I'm tricky to write for. I tend to be more cerebral, and not so obvious." Out of a thousand jokes wannabe joke writers send him, he may like only ten. The lucky jokester will get fifty dollars from Leno if the joke is one of the ten selected for use in Leno's routine.

Leno does celebrity jokes such as ones about Frank Sinatra.

"Frank Sinatra is such a big star that when he plays Las Vegas, all they've got to put on the marquee is 'Frank,' and everybody knows who they're talking about. Jerry Lewis is so big in France that when he's there, the ads simply say, 'The King Is Back.'" Pause. "I'm so big in Japan, they don't put anything in the paper. People open the paper, they don't see my name—they know I'm in town, and they rush to the club."

Or about Ted Kennedy.

"People laugh at Ted Kennedy, but how many other fifty-nine-year-old men do you know who still go to Florida for spring break?"

Or John McEnroe.

"A plane crashed in John McEnroe's backyard a few years ago. It's true. Well, McEnroe *says* it was in the yard. Officials say it was . . . on the line."

Then Leno's routine can veer back to one of his favorite targets, fast-food restaurants or their employees.

"They want us to call Kentucky Fried Chicken 'KFC' now. Why not call it 'CPR,' or 'DOA'?"

Since he likes collecting cars, he will also do gags about them.

"The weird names they have for automobiles these days! How do you get a woman to sit in a Ford Probe for the first time?"

His topics can be wide ranging. One minute he can be talking about books, such as *Final Exit*, the so-called suicide-assistance manual. "Libraries won't stock *Final Exit*. It just never seems to come back."

The next minute he's commenting on speed reading. "I heard that Evelyn Wood just lost a lawsuit. Yeah, a guy sued her because his eyeball blew out at ten thousand words per minute."

He will suit the topics to the audience, and unlike some of his comedian peers, he will take on audiences of all shapes and sizes.

He has friends who get a shot on a television show and someone on the show tells them, "Look, I love what you do, but there are certain things you just can't say on TV." And these friends say, "Hey, this is what I do. This is my art. Okay, pal? Thank you very much, good-bye."

People who don't make it, Leno says, are people who do material *they* like rather than material the *audience* likes. What gets Leno's goat are comedians who are playing a town like Oklahoma City and have the nerve to say, "So I'm taking the D train to the Bronx." The Oklahomans don't get it, and these comics come out with, "Hey, what's with you people? You're so unhip."

The truth is, Leno says, the audience isn't unhip. The audience doesn't know what the comic is talking about. The audience doesn't know anything at all about the D train and the Bronx.

"You hear about guys who refuse to play Vegas because they think it's so unhip and such schlock," Leno goes on. "I think that's a real snobby attitude. Everybody's got a sense of humor." It's a comedian's job to *find* it and exploit it, Leno thinks.

"I play Vegas. I put on a suit and tie and work. In Vegas they like jokes. Bing. Bing. Bing. You don't have to change your act, just your angles.

Leno explained to Tony Kornheiser of the *Washington Post* some of the things a typical Las Vegas routine might touch on. Remember that Vegas patrons are generally fairly hip to the entertainment business and the media. They are also quite up on all the various ins and outs of making money.

So, in the routine, Leno is at home one day, and he gets a telephone call.

"I represent Matt Lewis, an up-and-coming young singer," the caller tells Leno.

Leno says he's listening.

"You may not have heard of Matt," the caller goes on to say, "but he's about to embark on a nationwide tour of small clubs culminating in eighteen months with the Forum in Los Angeles and Madison Square Garden in New York, and he's looking for a comic to open up for him on the tour."

Aha. So this is an agent who wants Leno to go to work for him.

"What kind of money are we talking about?" Leno asks him abruptly.

"Before I get to that, Mr. Leno," the caller says, "let me say that *Time* and *Rolling Stone* are sending reporters on this tour with the intent of putting Matt on the covers of *Time* and *Rolling Stone,* and as Matt's friend and confidant you will, of course, share in this publicity and benefit from this attention."

Leno knows all that. "How much money are we talking about?" he asks, a little louder this time.

The caller clears his throat. "Not very much to start, I'm afraid."

Uh-huh. *"How* much?"

"To start, forty-five dollars per show"

Oh, my! thinks Leno. Why did he pick up the phone anyway? "My price is five thousand dollars per show," he explains patiently.

"Well," says the voice on the phone, "we can dicker on the price."

"Dicker? Are you kidding me?" Leno unloads on the guy. "What are we gonna dicker? You'll come up to fifty dollars, and I'll come down to four thousand nine hundred! Get out of here!"

And Leno *does* get out of there. By disconnecting.

Leno finds humor in almost everything around him—even modern movie theaters that have become "cement bunkers at the end of the shopping mall. . . . You drive twenty minutes to a five-thousand-acre parking lot, you walk half a mile to a cinder-block building. Fifteen movies are playing at once, each screen is four feet wide, they got sixty folding chairs, you feel like you're in some communist debriefing center."

Or even an ordinary circus can provide him a target.

"I hate the circus. Traveling syphilitic sideshow, these diseased animals and hermaphrodite clowns throwing anthrax spores at the children. This is like entertainment from the ninth century, geeks, trolls, mutants, all these inbred circus people—they come out from under bridges."

And what about the unicorn at this circus? "They got a goat being dragged around the ring with a Louisville Slugger stuck in his head."

Leno likes to identify the absurd in everyday life and milk laughs from it. He claims he is different from the absurdist Andy Kaufman, though. "People like Andy Kaufman are into the theater of the absurd. All they want is reaction from the audience. They don't care if it is a laugh or a howl of outrage.

"My comedy comes from reality," Leno says. "People used to laugh at ethnic jokes because they were uneasy or afraid of the unknown. Now they groan at ethnic stuff.

"Today's audiences are uneasy about high tech, nuclear war, and computers—the unknown—that's what they laugh at, the human spirit overcoming the technological age.

"They have to know where you're coming from, and they don't want to hear something they've heard before."

Corporations sometimes serve as grist for Leno's comedic mill. Their boners can lead to a bonanza of laughs. For example, long before the *Exxon Valdez* oil spill, Leno was going on about the oil companies.

"See what Arco has done? They've combined the all-night minimarket with the twenty-four-hour gas station to try to give you a one-stop robbery center. This way criminals don't have to drive around all night wasting gas. You pull in at nine-fifteen, shoot the attendant, and you're in bed by eleven."

Or take a variation of the same theme.

"Been to your local Mobil station lately? The station's owned and operated by Abdul Yashima. Guys are cooking dogs in the work bay. They're having a holy war with the Iraqi Chevron station down the street."

Leno admitted to a reporter that jokes about flying across the country invariably get a good laugh from his audiences.

"They say flying is safer than walking." Pause. "When

was the last time you saw an insurance machine in a shoe store?" Pause. "I always get stuck in the middle seat, between the screaming baby with diarrhea and the octogenarian with halitosis. We're like the three ages of man winging through time."

When George Bush was vice president, a little girl named Jessica McClure fell into a deep well in Texas. "She was doing fine," Leno reported, "but what an ordeal! In the well for fifty-eight hours—and then having to meet George Bush!" Pause. "It's enough to make her want to go back down."

Sociological statements of one kind or another are grist for the comedy mill. On May 25, 1987, Hands Across America attempted to raise funds for the homeless and the hungry. Leno's comment: "Is this how we achieve social change? Standing hip deep in the mud and holding hands with Robert Blake? Have we tried *voting?*"

Sociological, political—everything goes. Even jokes about Mayor Richard M. Daley.

"Most people who voted for his father are dead. Then again, most of them were dead when they voted for his father."

On Gorbachev's 1989 meeting with Fidel Castro, Leno said, "He was cheered by ten thousand screaming Cubans." Pause. "That was over Miami."

Despite the hours of writing that go into his jokes, Leno maintains that he is best at ad-libbing onstage.

"If you sit down and you write ten jokes, two of them will be funny. But if you're onstage, just ad-libbing to the audience, and you say ten things, probably seven of them will be funny, maybe eight."

About as controversial as Leno will get is a joke about the homeless.

"They get two meals, one at Thanksgiving and one at Christmas. Then it's, 'Hey, pal, you can't eat now, it's only July.'"

Or on the recession.

"I heard an economist on the news tonight. He said the recession is over. I guess he sold his house."

Some of Leno's favorite jokes are about his parents. These are love taps, reflecting his happy upbringing.

He once said he bought a TV and a remote control for his mom, and months later he visited her and found the remote control tucked away in a drawer.

"I was afraid to start a fire," his mother told him.

Leno: "She thinks it throws electric sparks across the room."

And then there's the one about his father:

"He won't get a hearing aid. He just figures if only Tom Brokaw and Peter Jennings would stop mumbling. When I drive to their house, I can hear the TV five exits away."

The ma-and-pa anecdotes strike Leno's audiences as the real thing. They are so real that everybody laughs heartily at them. His family jokes are gentle ones, nice ones, loving ones.

When Leno was sixteen, as he told it, he had just pur-chased a '34 Ford truck. He loved the truck and lavished all his spare time on keeping it clean and in smooth running order. Finally he earned enough money to have the seat reupholstered. Then, as luck would have it, he slammed the door too hard and shattered the window. By then he had used up all his money and couldn't replace it.

One day when he had the truck in the school parking lot, it started to rain. Of course, that was unmitigated disaster. The rain would ruin the brand-new upholstery. Leno was peering disconsolately out the school window wishing he could skip class and get the truck out of the rain when sud-denly he saw his mother and father pull up in the family car. He watched as they threw a sheet of plastic over the cab. Tears came to his eyes. His father knew how much the truck meant to him and had left work to protect it. There was always that strong bond between him and his parents.

How could Leno help but be nice with parents like that? They were fun parents—but they were caring parents, too.

The family might go to a wedding, for example. Leno would observe the disparate parts of his roots. The Italian side would be singing and dancing and eating—stuffing themselves. And the Scottish side would be looking at the Italian side in a kind of gaping wonder.

"Oh, look at them, Jamie, the way they carry on!" his mother might say.

The Italian side would be drinking and singing, and the Scottish side would be saying, "Would you like a warm Coca-Cola, Jamie?"

"It always amazed me that they would keep Coke and soft drinks in the *cupboard*," Leno observes. "The Scottish side was so stoic, the Italian so outgoing. It was always funny around the house."

His innate decency, learned from his parents, crosses over to people he has never met. Even when he is aiming jokes at real people in his audience, he tries to adhere to a set credo that acts as a subconscious guide for him, indicating whom he can poke fun at, and how much fun he can poke.

One. If the target is a lawyer, Leno considers him fair game. After all, it was Shakespeare who wrote: "The first thing we do, let's kill all the lawyers." Leno kills them with humor.

Two. If the target is a carpenter, Leno is more sympathetic. Here is a poor working slob without any clout. After all, he *does* build things. The barbs are much less cutting.

Three. If the target is an elderly person with a hearing aid, Leno sympathizes. Quite probably he may begin kidding him about his running shoes.

He has one golden rule:

He won't make jokes about *any* women. He assumes a firm stance on that. The best times in his life have centered around his mother and the women in his family—on both sides. What would be the point of making fun of women?

Even the women Leno dated before meeting Mavis Nicholson were all nice people. Since women played such an important and benign role in his life, he would be a hypocrite to make fun of them now.

Besides that, half the people who watch his show and enjoy his jokes are women. What would be the point of making snide remarks about them and getting them mad at him?

Leno knows that it is a tradition in humor to make fun of women and their ways—and has been since classic times—but he has made up his mind to avoid this kind of joke. If he began making fun of women, no one would think of him as Gentle Jay anymore. And they might begin to hate him.

Leno believes that audiences laugh more often at political jokes than at corporate jokes. In fact, Leno has gone on record on that score:

"I find people are more frightened by jokes about corporations than any kind of political joke. If I do jokes about Bush and Quayle, especially Quayle, they laugh, no matter how lame the joke.

"Sometimes I'll say, 'Oh, stop. It's not even that funny.' I did one about him last week. I said, 'It was Marilyn Quayle's birthday, and Dan took her to her favorite restaurant—Chuck E. Cheese.' They go, 'Whoooo!' 'It's not that funny! Now stop it!' I say. But you make fun of McDonald's or anything thought to be a corporate sponsor, and people will go, 'Oooooh.' I think they think you've gotten yourself in trouble."

Even with his genial nature and his care in not offending vulnerable people, Leno sometimes finds himself in a stressful situation—the same kind of stress all celebrities undergo from time to time because they are so constantly in the public eye.

One such instance occurred about six years ago. The story continues to surface in various versions—but the gist of it is contained in a recent *Chicago Sun Times* article by Cindy Pearlman.

Leno and his friend, Gene Braunstein, were riding their motorbikes on Mulholland Drive far above the city of Los Angeles along the spine of the Hollywood Hills. Leno parked his Harley-Davidson, and he and Braunstein stood up to stretch their legs.

It was dark, but the view of the twinkling lights strung across the immense Los Angeles basin was breathtaking. They were gazing at it enraptured when suddenly Leno felt the cold metallic thrust of a gun barrel pushed into his neck.

He tried to turn to see who it was, but dared not.

A voice sounded close to his ear. "You're trying to rob my house!" It was a male voice, poised on the edge of hysteria.

Leno tried to clear his throat. "What are you talking about? I'm riding my bike!" Honest indignation.

"You bikers are all thieves," snarled the man in the dark. Then he went on, beginning to shout, his voice rising uncontrollably. "You bikers are all thieves! A biker robbed my house last week!"

Apparently the man was not alone, for Leno could hear a woman speaking to him from a car somewhere in the dark. She was trying to get her husband to put away the gun and come back to the car.

The barrel pressed harder into Leno's neck. "I'll give you two minutes—you hear that?—two minutes to clear out of here and never come back!"

Then, as suddenly as the man had appeared, he was gone. Leno was left with only a stiff neck. Soon a car revved up and vanished in the dust.

Leno and Braunstein climbed back on their bikes and got out of there fast.

Six months later Leno was shopping at a swanky grocery store in Beverly Hills when he heard a voice calling to him.

"Jay! Jay! Remember me?"

Leno saw who was calling him. It was one of the shoppers. Leno had no recollection of the man.

"My wife yelled at me for pulling a gun on you!"

Now Leno recognized the midnight gunman.

"We saw you on television," the man continued, beginning to babble. "We're so excited that you were the guy I held at gunpoint!"

Oh, boy, thought Leno. Then—

"Hey! Would it be possible for you to *autograph* this box of cereal for me? Gee—"

The story has appeared in a number of different versions, including a November 1989 *Rolling Stone* article by Graydon Carter. In that version the punch line is not the hint that the man with the gun went to such great lengths to get an autograph, but that Leno was concerned about the fact that the man carried a gun.

"How about that gun?" Leno asked him at the end of the Carter version. "You still got it?" The story appeared in a *Reader's Digest* condensation of the same article, ending with the same words.

In the December 1990 *Playboy,* Leno told the story to Dick Lochte, but in that instance the anecdote came as the response to a question Lochte asked: "Everyone in show business has a strange story about someone seeking an autograph. What's yours?"

It's obvious that Leno is still trying to work out the proper punch line for the incident.

It'll come, Jay. It'll come.

Captain of the Comedy Ship Rule Number 54: *For every good buildup there's a great punch line.*

8

Love, Laughs,
and Lamborghinis

T HOUGH COMEDY is the love of Leno's life, his
wife, his motorcycles, and his cars run a close
second, third, and fourth respectively.

As for his wife's position *second* to comedy
and only a tad ahead of Leno's assorted motorcycles and cars,
the comedian has a standard rationalization:

"A lot of guys here in Hollywood have one car and a lot
of women. I have a lot of cars and one woman. It's a lot
easier."

The "one woman"—Mavis Nicholson, the daughter of a
character actor—doesn't seem to mind the fact that she takes
second place to her husband's love of comedy. After all, he
is faithful to her. When she calls him up while he's on the
road, it's Leno who answers the phone, not a sultry-voiced
woman.

For Mavis, who was brought up in the San Fernando Val-
ley, when she saw Leno at the Comedy Store, it was love at
first sight. At least, sort of. At that time—it was in the midseventies—she was trying to be a comedy writer, working
with two partners. Annoyed at having to write everything on
spec, she started to visit the newly opened Comedy Store in
an attempt to meet story editors and producers in person.

Mavis remembered the scene at the Comedy Store well.

"I was seated front-row center, with my nose practically on the stage, in the middle of this guy's routine. I'd never heard of him, but he was funny, tall, and kind of cute, and after seeing some of the other acts, I realized just how good he was."

Mavis's impression of Leno at the time: "He wore this snap-brim, scoop-ace-reporter-type hat, always a jeans shirt, a black-leather vest, a mother-of-pearl belt buckle, and tiny wire-rimmed glasses."

They met quite by accident that same night as they were both heading for the rest rooms after Leno's act. "And when I came out," Mavis said, "he was standing there."

"Say, you were in the front row," he said to her.

"Yeah, that was me," she told him, and breezed right on by. It was one of those unforgettable meetings etched in granite for both of them.

"He caught me by surprise," Mavis confessed. "When I don't have time to anticipate, I'm shy." But more to the point: "I also had a boyfriend at the time. But I thought he [Leno] probably would have been fun to know and chalked it up as a lost opportunity."

However, the next week Mavis chose to go to the Improv, another comedy club, which had an enormous plate-glass entryway window. Looking through the glass she saw a hat and thick black curls that seemed to float above the crowd. She saw a pipe and the smoke from it drifting above the heads of everyone else in the room. Fastened to the pipe was Jay Leno.

He had, she remembered, "the kind of hair most of us would die for." And then, of course, she realized it was the same man she had seen at the Comedy Store. "I thought, another chance."

A mutual acquaintance happened by and introduced the two to one another. They talked, laughed, became friendly.

"I have a tremendous passion for men who have blue

eyes, black hair, and large jaws," Mavis said. "We were each seeing other people at the time. But Jay was always very supportive. He was like that with everybody—kind, helpful, easy to talk to—but even though we were friends, there was always a little awkwardness, an underlying, unspoken tension between us."

In *How They Met*, a book about celebrities and their romances, Nancy Cobb described the two of them in her own words:

"Mavis and Jay Leno actually sound alike: similar speech patterns, similar timing. With tongue in cheek they approach life hand in glove, a bona fide team. Each is dark, one small, one large; each funny, and each the other's best fan."

According to Cobb, Mavis was approaching the end of her relationship and was finding the going difficult. Meanwhile, although she did not know it, Leno was also nearing the end of his relationship with the woman he was seeing. And so it was with a particular kind of astonishment that when Mavis finally revealed to him that she had broken up with her friend, he, too, said that he was through with his current romance.

"I was never much interested in marrying," Mavis confessed. "Before Jay, I had been attracted to a particular type of man: highly neurotic, unrelentingly verbal, extremely volatile. I couldn't even envision having a relationship with [anyone like Jay Leno] because he was their polar opposite."

The point was—opposites attracted, she thought. Opposites—and they were *not* opposites. "We're two peas in a pod emotionally . . . v-e-r-y s-l-o-w. So it snuck up on me when I realized one day what had happened. I was in love with him."

Mavis assumed she would never settle down with anyone. She always seemed to be traveling. It was as if there were a party going on somewhere, and she couldn't get to it.

"One day, I woke up and realized, I'm at the party. It's

Jay. He's the party. He's the destination. And it was the god-damnedest feeling."

Mavis once tried to put that feeling for Leno into words. "It was casual at first. We became great friends before we became romantically involved. It took a year before I realized he was the one. We moved in together."

Conversation with Leno was never like conversation with another woman—with no overshadowing hint of tension—but there seemed to be nothing immoderately false about their talks. Jay Leno was the only man she ever met, she said, with whom she didn't have to resort to her "bag of tricks" to keep a faltering conversation rolling.

"Being with him was like taking a vacation with a man." She could speak to him "person to person"—because he *listened.* Nothing escaped him. He paid attention.

She was reminded of an old aphorism: "Success doesn't change people. It just magnifies them."

Mavis believed that the secret of Leno's success in life was the fact that he was truly addicted to comedy. She knew that if she could make people laugh the way he did, there would be nothing else she would ever want to do either.

"Whenever I was with my girlfriends, we'd get into bitch-fests about guys. But I have no complaints about Jay. I have a great tolerance for being alone, and if he's out for a long time, I go with him. He's an equitable, fair man."

Mavis has a great resentment at being taken for granted, and just as much a resistance against taking anyone or anything *else* for granted.

"Is there something we should talk about?" she would ask Leno.

"Not really," he would say.

Mavis knew he was telling the truth.

"Living with Jay is one of the simplest things I've ever done. That's no easy thing."

As for Leno, he always maintained that he had never

been any good at the dating game. "I don't drink. I never have." He takes no drugs, not even aspirin. "I remember once Mavis wanted a drink, and the relationship almost degenerated on the spot."

"Look," Leno told her. "Let me give you the money, and you can buy a blouse or something. I don't want to buy you a drink."

He gave her thirty-five dollars and she bought a blouse.

Mavis on the incident: "I can't tell you how absolutely *peculiar* I thought that was."

Living together was a fulfilling experience for both the partners. They settled down into a companionable existence together in the comfortable ranch house Leno had bought in the Hollywood Hills. Their life together at home became one of books and bikes.

The books were essentially Mavis's way of life. She is, in Leno's terms, an "intellectual feminist." Reading is her greatest love. Leno was always astonished at the amount of textual matter she could consume in a day. However, it took her a day and a half to pour through *War and Peace,* he once noted with admiration. Her hobby was collecting books, concentrating mostly on late-nineteenth- and early-twentieth-century novels. Also the novels of Charles Dickens.

Motorcycles are essentially Leno's way of noncomedic life. Bikes and automobiles. As Leno once said of their relationship: "She has her literature and books and poetry, and I have my motorcycles and cars. I tinker, she reads. I'd be lonely if she weren't there."

Their lifestyles complemented each other. Their separate enthusiasms never seemed to come into conflict. Unlike many married males, Leno always respected Mavis's need for her space as much as she respected his need for his own. Somehow their differences justified the attraction they had for one another.

Leno had no intention of ever trying to *change* Mavis—

say, make her into a motorbike lover. Or get her to slow down on her reading. He has never been able to understand the urge certain people have to try to change their spouses into something else once the marriage has taken place. With Leno and Mavis—what they saw was what they got. And it made for a perfect combination.

Although marriage was not exactly in the offing at the point when they took up living together, it somehow lurked in the background. Asked about the moment when he finally decided to marry Mavis Nicholson, Leno was unable to pinpoint any particular moment in time.

The story he did come up with resembled one of his own routines. As he remembered it, he and Mavis had been together for a while. He was under the impression—a correct one—that she did not especially *want* to get married. One day, according to the story, Leno was paying a life insurance premium. He decided to read the policy carefully to make sure he had enough coverage; times were changing.

As he read through the ifs, ands, and buts, he realized he had a very comprehensive policy—to use the term favored by insurance mavens. In fact, he had a sheaf of policies, covering him for almost any untoward accident that could be imagined. It then occurred to him that, under his policies, Mavis was not covered for *anything*. He discussed it with her. She felt the problem was less than monumental. In short, she didn't care. But Leno was now convinced he had a way out. Legally, as a live-in companion, Mavis couldn't be covered by his policies. If they were married, then the policies could be rewritten to protect them both. It didn't sound like a terribly great idea to her. But finally, after thinking it over at her leisure, she agreed.

According to Leno, though, that was not the end of the story.

Leno's mother was happy to hear about his upcoming marriage; what mother wouldn't be? But when she finally winnowed out the details about the insurance policy, she thought it was the most hilarious reason in the world for any couple to get married.

In her words: "They got married because he had some policy." Laughter. A shaking of the head. "Mr. Skinflint. Mr. Tight Wad."

Finally, in 1980, the great day dawned, and the two of them were actually wedded. It was at the Kushnicks'—Leno's agent—that James Douglas Muir Leno and Mavis Nicholson tied the proverbial knot—in a six-and-a-half-minute civil ceremony.

In spite of the unromantic way their marriage seemed to have been inspired, Mavis had no doubts about its permanence. Nor did it surprise her some years later when *People* magazine called Leno "The Sexiest Man Alive" on the cover of a 1987 issue. It pictured the comedian smirking just underneath the headline.

Apparently few people got the joke: it was the second-lowest-selling copy of *People*. The lowest, incidentally, featured Charles Manson.

Leno's married life has broadened him considerably in the area of humanity and the human experience. Being with Mavis has forced him to see things and talk about things and to visit places he would not normally have.

Mavis confesses that she sometimes finds it hard to love a guy who has no faults. "I could count on the fingers of one hand the times he has said, 'I don't know what to do about this.' He's so complete in himself that it's frustrating, if you love him, to find something to give him, something he needs."

She tends to be a little grouchier than he is, but that's because Leno is pretty even-tempered all the time. Mavis gets bothered by people who ask him for autographs. "If she were the one who was famous," Leno says, "I think she would avoid it much more than I do."

As for Leno, he lays his satisfactory marriage to the fact that he learned a lot about women when he was growing up with his mother and his aunts on both sides of the family. But even that statement hides a punch line. And the punch line is this:

All the important women—the ones *he* considers important—were born on the *same date.* Not the same year, but the same *day.* The magic twenty-four-hour period for Leno lies between September 5 and September 6.

Mavis Nicholson was born on September 5.

"All the important women in my life were responsible, respectable—just good people," he says. "It was a very sheltered environment, emotionally. So I could never understand the way men talk about women, and I definitely couldn't understand the attraction of a dumb, insecure woman. You know this [male] thing of, 'Hey, that girl is real beautiful and plus—she's stupid!'"

Leno claims that he is one of those rather odd persons who tends to believe everything he sees, tries to accept things just as they are on the surface, and simply takes life as it comes for what it is. He also believes that opposites attract, that he is attracted to someone who doesn't accept things as they appear to be.

Perhaps the fact that Mavis and Leno both see themselves as different proves the fact the opposites *do* attract. Or perhaps this contradiction is only an apparent one. The real key to their attraction may lie in the fact that Mavis's birthday is September 5—Leno's magic day.

Playboy's Bill Zehme was present one night at the Leno home when Jay was counseling a friend who was experiencing marital problems. Leno had little patience with the man. Zehme wrote that Leno fired a series of questions at the man:

"How is she wearing her hair? When was the last time she changed it? What color are her eyes? When was the last time you *talked* with her—really talked? When was the last time you brought her flowers? Took her to the movies? Went out to dinner?

"You're being selfish! Hey, I'm not one of those I-love-you kind of guys. Nobody's home less than me. But you have to show *interest.* Tell her you've been selfish! Talk with her tonight. If not tonight, you'll never do it."

Leno is the picture of seriousness when he speaks of marriage. He is most specific about being frequently separated from his wife in his line of work:

"It's no different than if you're a salesman or in the service."

When he headed home from a gig, Leno telephoned his wife from the departure airport before he took off so she would know when he was due to arrive home. On the night he returned, they always talked at length before going to bed, bringing each other up to speed on the details of their separate lives.

As for Mavis, she rarely watched Leno's act. She rarely accompanied him on his road-show gigs. Leno explained why Mavis had chosen not to watch his appearances: *"That's how you keep a marriage together. I know wives who do accompany their husbands on the road. Their husbands make them sit there—and watch.* You see them, they're like a dog that's been kicked too many times. *Grrrrrr*—they just want the guy to die or to lose his vocal cords. They're sick of it. They just hate comedy."

Leno, of course, can't understand how anyone could hate comedy. He has described his job with these words:

"This is essentially piecemeal work. My whole day is free. I don't go to bed with worries about anything. It's fun. I work for no one. It's a bitch writing jokes every day. But when you do the show, it's as if you took a test and you got an A—then it doesn't seem like work at all."

Leno likes to contrast his job with that of a nurse or a cop. Of course, a nurse or a cop serves the community with a built-in good feeling about healing the sick and keeping law and order—but the rewards are inner, nothing tangible from the outside. No one cheers a nurse or a cop or claps hands over what the nurse or cop does.

With Leno, he might come up with what he considered his best joke ever. He would be on pins and needles waiting to get to the studio to deliver the line with his other jokes. And he wouldn't really be through until he tried it out—to find out if it was good nor not! Unless he tried it out on Mavis, who is his most severe critic as well as his greatest fan.

When Mavis first met Leno, she was not the least bit concerned that his career was going nowhere. She had the greatest confidence in him; she *knew* he would be at the top someday. It was simply a matter of time.

Nor did it annoy Leno either. He knew the ways of show biz. He knew about the twisting turns and the detours and the dead-end lay-bys. He had been in any number himself. Even so, his days were never grim or threatening. He was always on his feet.

While he may not have been an overnight smash, he had always enjoyed an easy ascent to fame. He never had to take other jobs to pay the rent. He always made enough from his comedy gigs to do that, except at the very start of his career in Boston when he was an automobile mechanic.

But those days of holding down two jobs at the same time didn't last long. He never had to wait on tables in Hollywood. A steady stream of money kept flowing in from his comedy gigs so he could devote all his life to improving himself in that one career.

Leno has confessed the narcissism of comedy attracts him. Maybe this explains why he would only see his wife three or four times a week and why they never planned on having children.

"There's a certain narcissistic appeal in what I do. It's the times we live in. Being funny is an asset. If I lived in the time of Genghis Khan, I wouldn't be doing this. I'd be dead by now. But I have to believe in what I'm doing. You make the product yourself. I work for myself."

For Shakespeare, the play was the thing. For Leno, jokes are the thing. Like the one about the recession:

"Saying we're in a slow recovery, not a recession, is like saying we don't have any unemployed—we just have a lot of people who are really, really late for work."

Then there's the classic Leno joke about oil companies and oil shortages:

"Whenever there's one of these bogus shortages, the oil companies give you those stupid brochures, *Fifty Ways to Save Energy*. They spill eighty million gallons in Alaska, and they want you to go to the bathroom in the dark and save three cents a year."

How can Mavis hope to compete with these jokes? Besides, she never expected to get married in the first place:

"To me, marriage seemed like the lowest circle of hell. But Jay comes from a traditional family, and I realized that he felt my living with him was less than being married to him."

Mavis is proud of Leno and can only say laudatory words about his legendary niceness. "Jay always goes that extra distance for people." He calls her three times a day when he's at work on the road. He's so nice he sent a videotape to Hattie Hannigan, an English teacher at Andover High School, which he attended as a child. On the video were greetings from sixteen stars—among them, Linda Gray, Debbie Reynolds, and Arnold Schwarzenegger.

The gigantic electrified gate in front of Leno's Beverly Hills, Tudor-style mansion isn't to keep people out, but, as Leno says, "to keep the starving guard dogs from straying too far off the property."

After Mavis on Leno's list of priorities come his motorcycles and cars, which he keeps in a warehouse-sized garage near his manse. He likes discussing his motorcycles on the "Tonight Show."

"Now, everybody has an opinion about motorcycles. Often on the 'Tonight Show,' I'll bring up the subject, and no matter which way the discussion goes, I'll get a lot of mail on the subject, most of it supportive."

Leno doesn't hang around with other celebrity motorcyclists such as Mickey Rourke, Dan Aykroyd, Arnold Schwarzenegger, Patrick Swayze, Sylvester Stallone, Gary Busey, or James Caan. Leno is a solitary cyclist, which is not surprising since he has always been a loner. When he was in college, everyone did drugs. It was a form of rebellion, but Leno rebelled against *that* rebellion. Likewise he now rebels against conformity and collectivism. He'd rather be an individual than part of a group.

Leno owns a Harley-Davidson FXRS Sport Edition, a Harley dresser, a Cagiva Paso, a Vincent Black Knight, and a Vincent Black Shadow. Each of these choppers has a V-twin engine, which Leno considers essential.

"V-twins have always been what bikes are all about," he says. "Aesthetically, for width, for handling, low center of gravity, the V-twin always was the ideal way to go. It's the perfect bike engine."

Posters and photographs of old motorcycles cover the walls of his garage. Letters from motorcycle clubs are thumbtacked to the remaining available space. The garage also boasts a hydraulic lift, which lowers motorcycles to the basement where Leno spends his leisure hours working on them.

He has restored Brough Superiors, a Honda CBX, a BSA, and a few weird midsixties Hondas. He doesn't like restoring Japanese machines. Problem is that when he gets them back into shape, they aren't worth anything. "I try to buy stuff that's worth something from the start."

Before he had millions of dollars, he had to collect cycles that he could afford. His four top-of-the-line motorcycles are a red-and-green Ducati Mike Hailwood Replica, a 750 MV Augusta Inline-Four, a 1970 Triumph Bonneville, and the crème-de-la-crème 1951 Vincent Black Shadow.

Leno claims the Ducati in action makes "one of the most beautiful sounds" a person can hear. He has nothing but praise for the Vincent Black Shadow, his favorite. Sometimes, when he needs to concentrate, he goes into the garage and just looks at it. There are all those little nooks and crannies to study. "I just don't think there is a prettier motorcycle than the Vincent. It's truly a classic shape."

Leno owns every issue of *Cycle World* magazine ever published. It was in that publication that he first read about the Vincent. The editors test-drove a ten-year-old Vincent Black Lightning and said it was a virtual death machine.

They soon heard from Leno by mail. "You guys said this was a death machine, and I'm only fourteen years old, so that's the motorcycle I've got to have." By the way, he told them, the Vincent guys were still mad about that test, especially that part where *Cycle World* called it an "evil-handling beast."

The first bike he ever owned was a Honda 90 when he was about fourteen or fifteen years old. Leno described its appearance:

"It was all busted up. It was in a field behind one of my friends' houses, and I think it had been thrown out by an angry parent or something."

Even worse, "it didn't run. I mean, half the parts were missing. Of course, being the master mechanics that we neighborhood kids were, we took it apart and painted the piston red and painted the block blue—just everything wrong. It never ran, but we had a lot of fun sitting on it, pretending it ran."

Later Leno got a motorcycle that did run. "My first year

in college I bought a secondhand [1970] 350 Honda from a Harley dealer. I used that for a while to get around until I could get a real bike."

The first bike he bought when he arrived in Los Angeles was a 650 Yamaha, which he now calls a piece of junk. When he used it, he said, he honestly thought he just didn't like to ride anymore. He felt that if this were it, he really didn't *like* bikes.

Leno saved up enough money to buy a Honda Inline-Six CBX. He loved that bike and rode it all over the place. Sure, it was a pain to work on, and it didn't handle, but it sounded great, and it was smooth and all the controls worked and the bike actually *stopped.*

"With my old bikes, when you wanted to stop, you had to get their attention first. It was like, 'Hey! Heyhey! Heyhey-hey! STOOOOOP!'"

What amazed Leno with the Honda was the fact that finally there was a motorcycle as technically interesting as any car. This inspired him to start collecting classic motorcycles. In 1977 he purchased the Black Lightning for four thousand dollars. He couldn't have been happier.

"I feel a special kinship with the Vincents." They just looked *right*, of course; it was a case of form following function. They were obviously designed by an engineer to work a certain way: the bike was one good man's vision of how a bike should be.

There were great stories that circulated about bikes when Leno was growing up. He was always hearing about "marvelous machines," but he never had a chance to see any of them in action. The old guys would tell him stories about how fast the Vincents were, for example.

Some guy would be racing another guy, falling down, and sliding a hundred yards right up to a saloon door. The rider would get up, dust himself off, wander into the saloon, and buy a drink.

"He comes out a few minutes later, picks up the bike," Leno says excitedly. "It fires on one kick and away he goes!"

There just aren't those stupid, wonderful stories with the new bikes, Leno notes sadly. And it's a mournful commentary on the difference between yesterday and today.

Leno takes pride in his restoration work on antique motorcycles. The great thing about the old bikes was to get one running properly, then keep it running long enough to get where you were going and back—*that* in itself was what gave you a sense of great accomplishment.

The newer bikes are too complicated for Leno and lack character. These bikes make cycling one big fat yawn:

"I think that one of the problems with motorcycling today is that people get bored." What is a guy with one of the new bikes going to do when he is finished riding it? Leno wonders. The difference between the new bikes and the classics is the same difference between a digital watch and an old vest-pocket watch hung on the end of a gold chain.

Leno can't get enough of the vintage machines. He loves the ritual of the old bikes: tracking down the brochures; hunting the original parts.

The idea that each old bike has a history appeals to him. "You can always associate a Vincent with the people who built it, much like people associate Harley-Davidsons with Willy G." Owning "one man's vision" turns Leno on.

Leno does all the maintenance on his motorcycles. Only when they have serious problems does he take them to specialists. "I do one thing well. I tell jokes, so when I have a serious problem, I take my bike to some friends. I'm almost embarrassed that I don't work with my hands when I am around these guys, because they are so *good* with machines."

Leno is no speed demon on his choppers. Once in a while, he has confessed, he does have his Walter Mitty moments with the bike when he goes zoom-zoom around a few corners and makes himself think he's going fast. "I feel so proud when I can get them running. I feel like I just won a road race."

A Hell's Angel Leno is not. Whenever he rides his motorcycle he wears leather and a helmet. Riding his bikes is the way he relaxes.

The new sport bikes have to be ridden fast, and that's another reason Leno prefers the older, slower models. He wants something he can ride down to the local post office. The old bikes fulfill this promise.

Leno is such a motorcycle nut that he once rode his Harley onto the stage of the Letterman show. Nice-guy Leno has also acted as ceremonial parade master for the Southern California Love Ride, which was a hundred-mile fund-raiser held for the Muscular Dystrophy Association.

For that parade Leno addressed the 1,300 motorcyclists with a contemptuous, "Yeah, if any of you guys are on *Japanese* bikes, don't worry, we'll have someone to help you out."

One of Leno's favorite bikes is his 1938 Brough Superior SS100. He calls it "the Brough," pronouncing it as you pronounce *rough*. It has a huge 1,000cc V-twin with double fishtail chrome pipes that flare out the right side.

Leno takes the Brough out every weekend. "I love going past some guys, going out to the Rock Store. I'll deliberately pull up along some guy on a Gold Wing, make a face at him, and pass him on the outside. Maybe it's because I'm in show business? That's the fun of owning the thing, *riding* it. I've put a lot of miles on the Brough. I take it to the club and park it on the street."

On Leno's toolbox is a brass plate with an inscription by T. E. Lawrence (aka Lawrence of Arabia) who rode Brough Superiors and even died on one. Says the inscription, "A skittish motorcycle with a touch of blood in it is better than all the riding animals on earth."

As he has for most everything, Leno has a story about motorcycles that he likes to tell.

"I had seen an article showing George Brough standing next to a Brough with chromed valve springs. I went, 'Oh, great.' So I chromed mine. Which you can't do, because of the hydrogen whatchamacallit. So I'm going down the highway one day and I hear *bping! bping! bping!* and all my valves went. I had to cut down new valves, get new springs. I went back and read that article carefully, and it said, 'Brough only chromed the valves for show models.'"

In other words, don't try this trick yourself.

Because riding a motorcycle can be dangerous, one network told Leno he couldn't ride a bike if he wanted them to put him under contract.

"I always ride my motorcycles," Leno said. "I work on them. This is what I do." He did not sign the contract. Of course, he lost some money, but why not? He figured he could always go to Des Moines on a gig and make it up there.

Admittedly Leno is not a tough-guy cyclist by any means.

"Well, the people I ride with are not stereotypical bikers. I mean, we don't go downtown and beat up homos."

One reason Leno moved from a Hollywood Hills ranch house where he first lived to his present mansion in Beverly Hills, just around the bend from Jack Lemmon's residence, was to find room for his raft of choppers and cars.

He owns a '67 and '70 Lamborghini Miura, a V-32 Packard V12, an '89 Bentley Turbo R, an '86 Countach, a '54 Jaguar XK120M, a 427 Cobra, a '46 Morgan three-wheeler, and of course, the infamous Buick Roadmaster, in which he had to sleep several times when he was a starving comic.

He likes each car for different reasons, depending on the mood he's in. "I just did the brakes on my Morgan, so I'm having a lot of fun with that right now. There's a car you don't have to be going ninety miles an hour in to appreciate."

As with motorcycles, he likes cars with character. He prefers a car that has its own special personality. In some cars, Leno believes, you can *see* the personality of its designer. "One guy *designed* that car, and his personality shows right through." Leno shakes his head, pointing out how different that is from the way a car is fabricated today by a "committee" system.

"I tend to like both Italian and British machinery," Leno says. An Italian car, he feels, has a feminine quality. "Italians try to cram as much horsepower as they can into their cars." He loves British cars, too, feels they are "charming" because they are so eccentric. Each British machine has a personality all its own.

"I guess what I've always loved about old cars, among other things, is they're primarily mechanical rather than electrical."

No matter what he needs to fix up his ancient Packard, he can go to a machinist and have it made.

"With these *new* cars, you've got a sealed black box that must be replaced by another sealed black box." Leno simply has no interest in that kind of thing.

He has always *enjoyed* working on a car. Since he makes his living primarily by talking, he can really appreciate working with his hands on mechanical things.

As an avid car collector, Leno has this advice for would-be collectors:

"Buy what you like. It costs as much to fix up a useless car as it does a classic. But even if it never skyrockets in value, you still have something you like. And you'll still enjoy it."

He says it's like looking for love. "You never find love when you're searching for it. Sooner or later though, it just turns up." However, when you're out trying to find it, and you don't find it, you have a *miserable* time.

Leno: "Go out to enjoy yourself. At least you'll have a good time."

When he and Mavis moved from their ranch house in the Hollywood Hills, Leno drove each vehicle in his collection to their Beverly Hills manse, and then Mavis drove him back in her Honda Prelude so that he could get the next car. This procedure took one entire day.

At three-thirty A.M., after Leno had moved his entire menagerie of vehicles, he returned to the ranch house, disinterred Mavis's dead cat in the backyard, drove the corpse up to the new manse, buried it there, slept for two hours, and arrived on time at the airport for his seven A.M. flight.

9

Money

L IKE ANY RED-BLOODED AMERICAN, Leno likes money. For him, comedy is a good way to make a lot of it.

"I've always been quite happy with my rate of success," he has said. "Even when I was twenty-six, twenty-seven years old, I was making about twenty thousand dollars a year, which, in those days, was fine. It was a lot of work, but that's all right. It gave me the opportunity to learn, to be bad without anybody knowing about it."

He admits it was tough economically for him at the very beginning. In fact, he felt like a whore. "I say that half-kiddingly. Being a comic is sort of like being a prostitute. When you start out, it's humiliating and degrading. But you get a hundred dollars in a half hour. And when you make money like that, you can't go back to doing something for three or four bucks an hour."

But the hardscrabble life didn't last long for Leno. "When you go out in the real world, where people work for a living," he said, "you tend to realize how easy the job of comedy is. It's not really hard. Not in relation to what it pays."

Jay has this to say about his job: "It's fun. But what's so unbelievable is that they are actually paying me money to have this much fun."

124

While he was guest-hosting on the "Tonight Show," which he did sporadically and then permanently from September 9, 1986, through May 22, 1992, he portrayed his income in the following manner: "The road is the principal and I live off the interest of the 'Tonight Show.'"

Comedy is Leno's business, so he looks at it with financial insight. This probably explains why he is so politically correct and so fretful about hurting anyone's feelings. A person who has been put out by a Leno joke isn't going to want to watch him. The lesson is obvious: Leno can't command big-ticket paychecks if he alienates too many members of his audience.

One time he did his headline routine on the "Tonight Show" and somebody complained about it. Leno recalled the incident:

"I read this headline to the audience about a guy who was decapitated. It said that authorities were still trying to determine the cause of his death.

"I thought it was pretty funny. I mean, you know, if a person's head is missing, the cause of death seems pretty apparent. Doesn't it?

"Unfortunately, the guy's family figured out who I was talking about, and they didn't see the humor.

"I called and apologized."

Leno's image goes to prove that political correctness is marketable, and in his case, marketable with a vengeance. For Leno, the money just keeps pouring in, enabling him to enjoy the coveted lifestyle of the rich and famous.

When you like your work as much as Leno does, what could be better than doing a job you enjoy and making oodles of money at it? It's hog heaven, and Leno knows it. Maybe this explains why Leno is so much at peace with himself— without the inner neuroses that other comics have, the comics that aren't quite so successful. And unlike other comics Leno doesn't have to psych himself up before appearing onstage. He just walks out and has a ball.

It's almost as if Leno is addicted to work. In *Vanity Fair*, James Wolcott wrote that Leno's fix is his fans. Unlike Johnny Carson, who used to keep fans at arm's length so they wouldn't besmirch his star quality, Leno is like a politician pressing the flesh out on the hustings. According to Wolcott, Leno can't get enough of his fans and for that reason will go to great lengths to avoid alienating them.

And it's not just job satisfaction that makes Leno tick; it's financial satisfaction as well. He works hard and he has become very rich while enjoying himself at the same time. One Saturday in a recent December he earned $25,000 working at a university in the day and another $30,000 at another college that night. When you consider he had nearly three hundred gigs a year before being selected to host the "Tonight Show," you can see this is a good way to become rich.

When asked what he does with the tons of money he brings home, he replied that he owns X number of motorcycles and Y number of cars. (The numbers change continually, usually escalating.) He then rattled off the makes of the autos: "a bunch of Lamborghinis, a Cobra, a Jaguar, a Bentley Turb." He went on, "I take care of my folks, my wife's family. I bought my father a car, my brother a car."

According to Leno's father, "Jay's only regret is that we already have a house. He would like to buy us one."

Sometimes, for Leno, it's hard to tell which is more fun—the "Tonight Show" or Vegas. However, he didn't *always* enjoy playing Vegas. In the seventies when he made his first appearance there as the opening act for singer Tom Jones, it was the opposite of fun.

What really ticked him off was the reception he got when he tried to buy tickets to his own show for a friend. At the booth Leno was told in no uncertain terms that Tom Jones did not even *have* an opening act.

"No. *I'm* the opening act," Leno retorted.

"Uh, sir, I don't think so," was the answer.

At that point Leno threw in the towel on Vegas.

"I didn't want to come back until I could at least head-line," he said. "I don't mean that in a snobby way. But I'd rather go to little teeny-weeny places where people come to see *me*."

Well, that was the way it worked out. For many years, Leno was flying all over the country doing his gigs, and yet he never took a vacation; he was having too much fun work-ing. Once he had eleven months of solid bookings and no complaints. In a five-day period he flew from New Hamp-shire to Toronto to Orlando to Santa Clara to Atlanta. Hon-olulu one day, New York the next. It was all the same to Leno. The raft of hours flying never daunted him.

"It's not *hard*," he explained. "Anybody making money in show business has no right to complain."

He insists that during the seventies and eighties he never went a week without doing at least one gig. If he didn't have a concert lined up, he'd work in a comedy club to stay in comedic shape. If he had ever deigned to take a vacation, he wouldn't have known what to do with it.

Leno respects his audience and listens to them. He told the *Los Angeles Times*, "When I saw Nancy Reagan do her 'Just Say No' number I didn't think much of it. But I called a friend who's a machinist. He said, 'Did you see the First Lady? That was really something.' He made me rethink my perspective."

Fred de Cordova, then executive producer of the "Tonight Show," once called this anecdote an indication of Leno's "innate sense of taste."

To him, working is his recreation. He never takes a rest. He considers hard labor his fun in life. It annoys Leno that people are uniformly appalled at his dedication to such important values.

"This must be the first time in American history when it's

considered strange to work hard! I don't want to sit on a beach! This is what I do! But people think there must be something psychologically wrong with me."

Leno was struck by another difference between the two Coast cultures when a recent interview of his appeared in *Rolling Stone* magazine. "In Los Angeles," he said, "they want to know where you were *positioned* in the magazine. In Andover, it's, 'Wow! *Rolling Stone.*' They're impressed if you even have a *subscription* to it."

Leno is so happy with his job and his life that he cannot in his wildest dreams imagine doing anything else at all. When asked what he wanted to do five years from now, he said, "Exactly what I'm doing now! I don't understand why no one wants to be doing what they're doing. Actors want to sing, singers want to act. But people are annoyed when I say that. Like, somehow, I should want to take up modern dance."

Even with that packet of money in his pocket, Leno never flaunts his wealth on the road. Unlike Eddie Murphy and other celebrities, he does not travel with an immense entourage of flunkies serpentining after him through airports and hotel lobbies. He prefers to tote his own luggage. "I don't like having handmaidens."

Leno won't eat at expensive gourmet establishments either, but selects a restaurant for its view of the parking lot. He likes to be able to see his car to make sure the lot attendant keeps his hands off it. After all, food is secondary to transport in Leno's eyes. Whereas other Hollywood luminaries can be seen at Spago or Morton's, Leno never patronizes them. They don't jibe with the regular-guy image he projects.

"I'm more likely to be seen at Tail o' the Pup or Hard Times Pizza. Maybe Marino down on Melrose. Or Santo Pietro in Beverly Glen. I'm not real fancy. I'm on the road so much that when I get home, eating out isn't all that important.

"I've finally gotten to the point where I tell people I'd rather just meet them *after* dinner. I guess I've reached that level of success where I don't *have* to go to dinner anymore.

"Anyway, I really come from the stand-over-the-sink world of eating."

Regarding food, he once said, "I still enjoy watching extravagant lifestyles more than being a part of them. When I was living in New York trying to be a comedian, I'd go to the Stage Deli, where a roast-beef sandwich cost four dollars and fifty cents. I couldn't bring myself to spend four-fifty on a sandwich, so I'd get a hamburger for a dollar ten."

Back there with his wife recently, he said, "Let me show you where I used to hang out." He took her to the Stage and told her how he could never allow myself to buy a roast-beef sandwich because it cost four-fifty, but that now he was finally going to *get* that sandwich! Well, when the menu arrived, it was marked at *nine*-fifty!

"I'm not paying nine-fifty!" Leno shouted. "It used to be only four-fifty!" Pause. "I didn't want it *that* much."

Leno has another set piece about the hazards of dining out if you're rich—especially if you're rich *and* famous. The set piece revolves around a night in which the Lenos quite uncharacteristically eat in Atlantic City at a swank French restaurant. During the meal a hardworking waiter sweating over a flambé nearby recognizes Leno as a well-known personality and shouts across the flames:

"Hey! You're da fuckin' guy! Right?"

The Lenos sink slowly through the floor with embarrassment, as the sophisticated patrons all turn to stare at them in horrified disbelief.

Though he makes millions, Leno is tight with his money, especially when it comes to food. On the other hand, when it comes to cars and motorcycles, money is no object.

Leno often shakes his head at the innate dishonesty of TV when it trucks with money, particularly in a story-line and plot sense. He remembered watching an episode of "Fantasy Island" in which a happily married man began to imagine how good life would be if he had a million dollars. In the show, of course, he *got* his million through some wildly imaginative plot mechanisms. Once rich, however, he immediately underwent a character change and turned into what Leno characterized as "Joe Prickhead."

Prickhead became bored with his wife and family and took off, turning into a part-time womanizer and part-time stuffed shirt. And so the marriage headed for self-destruction. The man was on the verge of divorce when . . .

Enter Ricardo Montalban: "Do you know that money is not often the key to happiness?"

Not so unbelievable so far.

But then—

Prickhead was so genuinely affected by Montalban's sermon on the fantasy mount that he ascended the heavens to instant sainthood by taking the dirty old money and throwing it into the river. There was, of course, a convenient river on the "Fantasy Island" set for just such a sacrifice. As soon as the cash sank out of sight, the guy and his wife became poverty-stricken but happy again.

In Leno's eyes, the fable was simplistically stupid. He cut to the heart of the matter:

"I'm convinced that certain facts of life are disguised by the powers that be to keep poor people from seeing how much fun it is to be rich. I mean, I've been broke and I've had money, and it's a lot of *fun* having money."

No one's basic nature changes with the acquisition of wealth, Leno says. "Why should I be a sudden prick now that I have a few bucks put away?"

He recalled another example of the idiotic way TV treats money, this one in a commercial. The commercial deals with an English guy who is looking very aristocratic and is speaking in a flawless Henry Higgins accent:

"Here's a priceless introduction to the classics that will enrich every home," he announces. The picture shows a posh London flat. There's a grand piano, a candelabrum, a bust of Beethoven, a harp, a bright painting of a fruit bowl mounted in a gilt-edged frame, red drapes, and Victorian sconces on the wall. But the total effect desired is negated by the fact that all these earthly goodies are crammed into a *tiny square space* about the size of a postage stamp.

As Leno points out, the so-called country-house concept is really nothing more than a bum's idea of how rich people live. Ordinary people cannot conceive of having a lot of space, so they just figure that the other half lives in the same little rooms they do, with all of these expensive furnishings stuffed inside. To Leno, "It's the funniest commercial on TV."

Even though Leno is a millionaire many times over, he claims that he lives a relatively simple life. He and his wife have a house in Beverly Hills. "There's almost enough room for us and my cars and motorcycles," Leno says, with tongue only partially in cheek.

To illustrate the "simplicity" of it all, Leno has a set piece he tells. In the set piece he and Mavis take a bottle of champagne to the people next door to introduce themselves. A maid appears; the neighbors aren't home. But the maid is civil and asks the Lenos if they have a full or half staff. Leno pretends not to understand, but Mavis jogs him. Leno answers something to the effect that they have only a half staff now—but the hint is, later they may have a full staff.

This is a carefully constructed story that reflects Leno's nice-guy image. But note that it subtly exhibits a reverse snobbery against the nouveaux riches next door. The story, of course, puts a different twist on the "simple life" Leno purports to live.

Leno resents the prevalent idea that comics *should* be poor. He doesn't know who got this notion started.

When he was a kid, he used to read about a comedian who was making a lot of money—a comedian who was so cheap he'd take the shampoo from his hotel room away with him. But now Leno sometimes finds himself taking the shampoo—because the way things are today, maybe the next place won't have any!

Leno knows the value of money. The money he makes he puts in the bank and uses it to pay his taxes. He thinks of money in terms of how much of it he has in his pocket. That was part of Johnny Carson's appeal, as well.

"People will tell me they spent a hundred and twenty dollars on a meal in a restaurant, and *I'll* be genuinely shocked," Leno admitted. Just like Carson.

It bothers Leno when certain writers make an issue of his wealth, as though comedians aren't supposed to have a lot of money. The only reason Leno can think of is this:

"I don't really lead a particularly exciting life. My wife and I have been together for twelve years [in 1989], we've been married for nine, and I don't show up in certain places or have affairs or anything. So I imagine that's a hook.

"I have never, ever said in an interview what I make or how much I got for a particular job. I don't call myself a millionaire comic. It's very embarrassing. I work exactly as hard if not harder than I ever did when I wasn't making any money."

When it comes to his parents, Leno is not at all closefisted. He bought his father an extremely expensive car. When they got to the car dealer's, Leno ordered them to bring out the biggest and most expensive model they had in stock. It was so costly that the sight of it caused all the Scottish blood in his mother's body to rush to the surface in her cheeks.

Leno admitted later that the car looked like Elvis Presley's coffin. It was a bright white on the outside, upholstered inside with a red velour.

Catherine Leno's dead ancestors whispered warnings

down through the centuries into her ears. She felt herself shudder at the messages. "It's too *flashy!*" she cried to Leno. "People are going to think we're in *Who's Who.*"

"Just ride in the car," Leno told her patiently.

She did—not without misgivings. When nothing untoward happened, of course she calmed down and accepted the good fortune of her son. And admitted later that it was fun to have a rich and famous celebrity in the family.

Leno may not like to speak about how much he makes, but as of 1991 he was reportedly earning more than $3 million a year by one account, and $10 million by another. In May 1992, when he took over the "Tonight Show," he was suddenly required to keep a grueling five-nights-a-week pace to earn his millions—unlike Carson, who only worked three days a week and had a three-month vacation every year. Leno was quite abruptly required to put in a five-day workweek like everybody else. He had to work forty-nine weeks a year, with three weeks off for vacation.

Leno is proud of his contract with NBC. He told an interviewer, "If I'm gonna work, I might as well work every night.

"The problem with network TV is too many reruns. Everything falls into a pattern and becomes predictable. So I figured, why not do new shows every night, at least for a while? Johnny did it that way when he was first starting out."

Leno can handle the pressure of the nightly grind. "It's like sitting on a pot of boiling water. All you've got to do is keep the lid on.

"My career is sort of like watching the hands of a clock. They don't appear to move until you come back a year or two later and you go, 'Oh, look!' People forget I've been doing this for twenty-one years."

10

The Conversationalist

W HEN LENO WAS GUEST-HOSTING the "Tonight Show" during his once-a-week gigs, he would rattle off one-liners in his monologue in nanoseconds, but as a matter of fact he always built his comedy routines around little stories he used to tell—stories that he knew were surefire laugh getters.

As an interviewer on the "Tonight Show," the first thing he learned was to keep the show moving with fast, short ad-libs after the guest had had his say. As an interviewee, on the other hand—for example, when he would guest on the Letterman show—he would once again revert to story-telling out of the deep bag of comic tricks he had assembled over the years.

Once he became installed as permanent host—and star of—the "Tonight Show," Leno made some specific and telling changes in his style. He also retained some specific and telling familiars. The one-liner, for example, continued to serve as his primary weapon.

"I never used to be a one-line comedian, but on 'Tonight,' there's no time to tell involved stories." He adapted that element of his routine to his new status.

When asked how he would keep in touch with the rest of

America after he became the host of the "Tonight Show"—thus forcing him to curtail his traveling—Leno responded with these thoughts:

"After you've been doing this for twenty years, you learn to go with your instincts. You know when you've done one Quayle joke too many. I meet the 'Tonight Show' audience before the show. And don't forget, when you do a monologue every night, you can *feel* an audience's reaction, pro or con. They give you a sense of what's appropriate and inappropriate. Johnny Carson can still read an audience better than anyone."

Now that he is permanent host, Leno feels morally obligated never to embarrass the "Tonight Show" in any way. "When you think of some of the horrible things this country's been through—the assassinations of John F. Kennedy and Martin Luther King, the Vietnam years—the fact that Johnny was able to get up night after night and find comedy in the day's events or find some way to make people laugh was an amazingly hard thing to do.

"Let 'Nightline' handle the crises and Donahue ask the probing questions. On 'Tonight' you want to have the light side. I hope it never changes."

Some Hollywood observers believed that it took Leno a long time to get regular hosting jobs on the "Tonight Show" because he didn't *look* like a Midwestern WASP. These observers must never have watched the show. How many Robert Redford–type comedians have hosted the "Tonight Show"? Joan Rivers? Garry Shandling? In fact, how many Midwestern WASP comedians are there, anyway, besides Johnny Carson? If they're out there, they are rarely seen on television.

In any case, Leno always intended to keep the monologue on the "Tonight Show." To Johnny Carson this was always *the* favorite six minutes of the show. To Leno it was an integral part of the menu.

Leno had no intention of changing the set much. A couple of chairs, a desk—what more can you do with a talk-show set?

He had planned to interview guests who would be somewhat *different* from Carson's usual selections. Carson's choices tended to be movie stars. Leno wanted to interview more ordinary people, especially those who happened to be in the news because of what they did or because of what they would do, or perhaps, because of what they had *refused* to do or even *failed* to do.

Interestingly enough, when Leno and the top brass finally got together their list of guests for the first week of Leno's reign in May 1992, the selections were in no way fundamentally different from the past. Here are a few of them:

Billy Crystal. Crystal had made himself a household name with his recent appearances as host of the Academy Awards and had appeared in a blockbuster "Western" movie that was a sleeper hit.

Tom Cruise. Cruise was a regular heartthrob of all young American moviegoers.

Mel Gibson. Gibson was a favorite with almost everyone—his Australian background adding just a slight fillip to his engaging personality.

Emilio Estevez. One of the talented acting sons of Martin Sheen, Estevez was an excellent draw at the box office; what was more, he was also critically acclaimed.

Well, how different could you get without disappearing from the ratings charts in toto?

Leno would not make anywhere near the $25 million a year at the job the way Carson did, but he would come in at $3 million a year—and that ain't hay.

He would adhere to his favorite comedy topics and would probably do a lot of TV jokes, à la Carson.

"I always contend that you can make fun of TV and think it's stupid and still watch it," Leno said. "I always get annoyed at the type of performers who make fun of things from above. You can make fun of TV from within.

"Just because I go to a fast-food restaurant doesn't mean I can't make fun of fast food. And it's the same with television. You can watch it and still think it's stupid and tear it apart." With humor, of course. With a twinkle in the eye.

One expected to hear on Leno's "Tonight Show" jokes like the one Leno made long ago about the "most embarrassing" show on television—which he felt to be the annual "People's Choice Awards":

"I don't know who these 'people' are, but they should have the freedom of choice taken away from them. You can see where the education in this country is going from the fact that Robert Blake and Mr. T can beat out Sartre and Descartes for Best Philosophers on the 'People's Choice Awards.'"

Leno himself always preferred the cerebral comedy of Bob and Ray, Mort Sahl, and Bob Newhart, which involved long, intricate stories that eventually led to a punch line. However, he knew that, because of a TV audience's short attention span, he had to concentrate on one-liners when he became host of the "Tonight Show."

One-liners like the famous one about the expiration date on Wonder Bread:

"Hey, pal—you should live so long!"

Or the one about 7-Eleven stores where "twenty thousand dollars worth of security equipment guards twenty dollars' worth of Twinkies."

And for sure one could count on Leno to continue doing his patented Elvis Presley jokes:

"They now have undeniable truth that Elvis is really dead. It is the most conclusive proof yet that Elvis *is* actually dead. It turns out yesterday he registered to vote in Chicago, so he *must* be dead."

In his "Tonight Show" monologue, Leno would not be able to do the long, complicated stories he once did concerning Elvis Presley. For example, he once told an Elvis joke to an interviewer who brought up the subject:

"I've always been an Elvis fan. I've gone to Graceland. Since I'm from New England, there's nothing I enjoy more than seeing a Chippendale dresser that's been painted purple and orange."

Leno told the reporter that he had met people who were convinced Presley was still alive and pumping gas somewhere out in Idaho. You could not really blame them, Leno pointed out.

"I saw a magazine not long ago that had a big picture of him on the cover, with the caption reading 'Elvis at Fifty.'"

Leno saw people picking up the magazine, staring at it, and muttering, "Jeez! He looks *great* for fifty!"

It was crazy! "Elvis doesn't look *great!*" Leno said. "He's *dead!* He's *dead!*"

It took forever to get to the punch line of this particular Elvis story; it seemed to wander about a great deal before finally getting there. An ordinary TV audience would have switched channels instead of waiting for the snapper.

The first Elvis one-liner—about registering to vote in Chicago—always worked better on TV since it grabbed the listener's attention immediately.

In regard to specific celebrities Leno would have on his show, he planned never to hype anybody's work he didn't truly like.

When he was doing his guest-host gigs on "Tonight" he never bothered to. Recently, during his guest-hosting stint, one of his guests was Jackie Collins, the writer of Hollywood sex potboilers and sister of the actress Joan Collins. Jackie became teed off when Leno told her off-camera that he hadn't read her current book because he couldn't stand the genre.

"I told her I was sure she was a very nice person and I would hold up the book, but I was not going to say, 'My next guest is a wonderful writer.' It's like Harold Robbins. He is *not* a good author. He writes *Penthouse* letters that are very long. It's stupid. I hate it."

Unlike Letterman, who will insult the guests on his show willy-nilly, Leno will not, though he may have some unflattering words for them, as in the case of Collins—and off-camera at that. Leno is not an adversarial interviewer. He doesn't believe in putting any guest on the hot seat.

He has his own private theory of interviewing. "I think that as TV enters the nineties, people would rather watch somebody with an opinion, even if they don't agree with it. We've reached a point where PR has become such a science that when people are pushing something, they know exactly what to say to hype it. When you get somebody with an honest opinion—then it makes the talk *real.*"

To be a good host, Leno believes, you have to ask questions that an average person would ask.

"I like show business, and I'm as interested in it as most people, but I don't live here." He meant he was usually on the road and not physically in Hollywood. "So I don't already know the answer to the question I'm going to ask."

Leno's idea about being a good host is exemplified by the time he had homosexual playwright Harvey Fierstein on the show and, confessing interest in the homosexual lifestyle, asked:

"I don't mean to be odd, but what's a gay guy's opening?"

"I was being totally honest," Leno explained, "and I wasn't making fun of his lifestyle or anything, and I got letters from gay people saying thanks for asking the question. To me, that was something people would honestly like to know the answer to."

The five-nights-a-week schedule never bothered Leno. He always looked forward to working at the thing he liked best to do.

"When Johnny started, he did five nights for an hour and forty-five minutes. People joked about his schedule, but he certainly earned the right to do three nights a week. I figure the least I can do is try and work at least as hard as Johnny had to do the first few years."

Just before taking over the show, Leno found that he could hardly wait to start in on the new schedule.

"It's a big deal, but I'm not someone who runs an emotional gamut on things. I don't get horribly depressed or get giddy and jump around like a schoolboy. But you start thinking, 'Oh, gee, now I've got the ball, and I can't drop it.'"

Leno had perfected a marvelous style as a guest comic—a technique that may be lost now that he has taken over the reins of host-interviewer. In contrast to his "Tonight Show" monologues—the one-liners—he perfected a nice easygoing raconteur style of humor, telling long, involved stories with brief chuckles interspersed in the buildup, and ending with a big laugh.

For example, on December 12, 1991, Leno appeared as a guest on the Letterman show to plug his new book, *Headlines III: Not the Movie, Still the Book.* Letterman and Leno engaged in friendly banter about Leno's new job—he had not yet taken over the "Tonight Show," of course.

Letterman wondered aloud if Leno was feeling any pressure about that approaching takeover. Although the chatter was innocuous, an underlying tension between host and guest was obvious. That had to be, of course. The feelings between the two had not been entirely ironed out yet by the public relations corps at work on it.

Pressure? Leno thought about that. He hemmed and hawed. Then, arriving at the proper point, he grinned. "I got some money in the bank." If he blew the job, he simply blew it. He'd be all right, no matter what the outcome.

The chatter then turned easily to a very recent event—the rape trial in West Palm Beach of William Kennedy Smith.

Half the TV sets in America had been tuned in to the courtroom scene during the daytime hours. For those at work when the sun was up, nighttime news carried all the interesting facets.

Leno was particularly interested in one detail that surfaced at the trial. In discussing women's underwear, he noted, women used the word *panties* freely and easily and without embarrassment. However, when the men were handing around the woman's underwear, they would always call it "underwear," and never "panties."

Why? Leno wondered. Why were women able to say "panties" without embarrassment, but men seemed to feel that the term would appear lascivious?

No conclusion was reached, but the audience chuckled appreciatively.

Leno then moved on to a more involved and extended story about visiting a delicatessen in New York City to sample the ethnic food. The point involved a misunderstanding about not putting sour-cream sauce on his hero sandwich, with the proprietor taking it out on his son—physically.

The flavor of the story was in the buildup. Of course, an anecdote of that length would have died if Leno had put it in the framework of a "Tonight Show" monologue. That audience was programmed never to wait for a punch line arriving by slow freight. Leno, as Letterman's guest, sitting down, could get away with a wandering tale because he had no compulsion to milk a laugh a minute out of the audience. As a guest, he could do the relaxed slow-mo routine.

After some more talk, Leno went into a long joke about his mother, one of his favorite comedy subjects. In the story, Leno telephoned his mother from Colorado Springs where he was appearing for a gig. In describing the place to his mother, he casually mentioned the place where he was appearing: "Pike's Peak Theater."

His mother understood "Pike's Peak," of course—from

the TV show. After the typical misunderstanding between "Pike's Peak" and "Twin Peaks" was milked to the bone, Leno simply shrugged it off and let his mother continue in the dark.

Again, this was a long joke that would never have fitted into Leno's "Tonight Show" format. He also did a shorter joke at the end of his Letterman appearance that *might* have worked in a monologue.

He was on the telephone to his mother again. This time he was in New York, and she was in Boston. About to ring off, he mentioned that it was eight o'clock. His mother: "Here it's five to eight. I guess it's the time difference."

On balance, maybe this joke would take too long for a "Tonight Show" monologue, too. However, it went over very well on the easygoing Letterman show.

It is instructive to note in passing how much Leno depends on the humorous device of "misunderstanding" for his family and personal anecdotal material. Of course, historically, the misunderstanding is the basis of all farce and dramatic comedy. He draws from a classically sound tradition.

What Leno needs for his stand-up monologue is something short and snappy, such as one of his KFC jokes.

"Kentucky Fried Chicken wants to be called KFC. They don't want 'fried' in their name. They *should* take out 'chicken.'"

Leno would be the first to admit that his monologue jokes have lost some of their freshness and punch over the years.

"I think the criticism is fair. But hosting the 'Tonight Show' is a lot like running for the Supreme Court. You have to please a lot of people to get there, but once you get there, you get to do what you want."

He is bound and determined to invite deep-thinker guests to his show, rather than "women who slept with Steve Garvey."

Leno will also continue to do political humor as he eases into his spot on the "Tonight Show," and the humor will not be preachy.

"All you do with comedy is reinforce what people already know," he has pointed out before. Know, or think. "You don't change anybody's mind. People have to sort of agree with you to laugh at your joke, otherwise they just go, 'Oh, that's wrong.' You only have a lot of power until you try to wield it.

"I think people will laugh because they trust you. I'm someone who does not have his picture taken with any candidates. I don't show up at fund-raisers. So I can't be accused of being on one side or the other, although I often am."

The trouble with topical humor is that you can jump ahead of the audience and they won't laugh at the joke. Leno believes that it takes people a full day to sort of ingest something to the point that you can make a joke about it.

"Like, I had a bunch of jokes the other week about Donald Trump going out with that Italian model. I put the monologue together, and *that day* Trump announced he was engaged to Marla Maples.

"So I took those jokes out, and that night I did a couple of jokes about him being engaged to Marla, and I could sense the studio audience didn't *believe* me. They've been on vacation, they've been waiting in line all day, and they said, 'What?' It didn't get much of a laugh. Whereas the next night it *did*, because they *believed* me. They'd heard it in the news."

Leno makes no bones about it. He admits he was lucky to land the "Tonight Show" job.

"It's an odd sort of situation, and I've been very lucky up to this point in that when I started hosting the show, no one ever said to me, 'Okay, listen, you're going to have to have a certain amount of ratings,' or, 'Jay, we've checked your demographics and you're very low with immature men between eleven and fourteen.'

"I was just expected to come in here and fill in, do the best I could, and don't worry about anything. So I figure I got the job with that attitude, I may as well continue with that."

Leno doesn't plan on blowing his brains out if the "Tonight Show" sinks with him at the helm. He doesn't need a TV gig to earn his livelihood.

"I've always made a living without television. I mean, television helped augment it, in the sense of saying, 'Well, I'll be playing somewhere tomorrow,' that type of thing. But I've never had the sort of career that if television ended tomorrow, I would be out of a job.

"Like, Jack Paar is essentially a television performer. Jack never had a nightclub act, as far as I know. So when TV ended, then you're gone. With me, you say, 'Well, okay, I guess I'll go back on the road, do the clubs, and hopefully work Vegas, and see what happens.'"

Leno doesn't plan to halt his road gigs as he puts in his five-day workweek on the "Tonight Show."

"If you're not out on the road, if you have no contact with the public, you might do the show one night and have no idea why the ratings are down. You have to go out on the road and just sort of listen while you're signing autographs, hear what people have to say, or see what gets a laugh."

His road gigs used to act as a barometer for his "Tonight" work, indicating success or failure with the public at large.

During his stint as guest host Leno explained, "I mean, I come in here and do the 'Tonight Show' during the week, then I go out on the weekends and find out what people like. If someone says, 'Oh, I didn't like that interview you did with so-and-so, I thought you were mean to him,' and I'll go, 'Really? Jeez, I thought I was being funny.' Now I know when to lighten up, or 'Why didn't you go after this guy harder?' People tell you what they want."

Also, touring is the way you can keep your head screwed on right.

"If you go on the road and you're in a twenty-five-hundred-seat auditorium and all twenty-five hundred seats are sold, well, you must be doing *something* right. If only three hundred seats are sold, you're probably doing something wrong. That's really the way you have to judge it."

Leno is always interested in audience reaction to his material. Some of the reactions can be pretty wild and throw the barometer all out of kilter. Leno described one such incident in this manner:

"I got a letter once from a guy that said, 'Dear Mr. Leno: You attack our vice president, Dan Quayle. What's your military service? I'll bet you never served in a war,' and on and on. He's a retired captain in the U.S. Army. And I thought, 'Oh, that was nice of him,' so I call this guy up, and we talk a little about Quayle, I explain why I do certain jokes, the vice president's office has always been humorous, blah, blah, blah.

"So about two weeks later, I get another letter and I say, 'Oh, retired captain, it's that guy again.' I open the letter, and out falls a picture of him and his wife, both in their seventies, full frontal nudity, inviting me to come and stay with them in their nudist group.

"And it says, 'Dear Mr. Leno, Hope you're not offended by our nakedness, but we got along so well in our conversation . . .' So it's real funny. My favorite people are the ones who seem normal and then after about five minutes I realize they're not."

Leno's sensitivity to others is reflected in his role as interviewer. Although he never set himself up to be an interviewer when he started out in show business, he learned a lot from being a guest and from watching how his host or hostess handled him.

After Christmas in December 1991, Leno had the former professional football player for the Minnesota Vikings, Ahmad Rashad, as a guest on the "Tonight Show." Even though Leno detests organized sports of any kind, he did not allow any of his umbrage to show when he questioned Rashad. He was always polite and gentle.

The talk drifted around to children—Rashad had five—and the football star asked the normal follow-up question. Did Leno have any?

"No, I don't," he answered quickly. "Maybe after the show tonight."

Leno is sensitive about discussing these details on the air, but in this case, he had seen that the audience was beginning to doze at Rashad's colloquy on his kids. His joke served two purposes: it saved Leno from questions about children; and it turned the conversation into more interesting channels once again.

Jay Leno's sit-down interview style is quite similar to his stand-up comedy style. He tends to simper just a little, but not excessively. He is not a contender the moment the talk starts; if anything, he is sympathetic and understanding. Also, he knows how to listen. His best remarks are the result of something a guest will say—not straight up from the floor on his own.

"The key [to a good interviewing style] is to listen to what people say, for something to turn around," Leno told Elvis Mitchell in an interview printed in the *Fresno Bee*.

For example, one night Leno had John Davidson on. "I do the 'Miss World Show,' but it means nothing," Davidson said.

Leno thought about that. It was something that had seemed to slip out of Davidson's mouth, but its implications jangled warning bells in Leno's mind.

"Oh," he said, rearing back a little and looking at the singing star intently. "So you're doing *this* because it means nothing." A statement, not a question.

Davidson caught the drift, reddened, flustered, but the

interview continued. Leno had him dead to rights on that one.

Although not adversarial, Leno has his scruples and enough quick wit to leap at any loophole that chances to present itself.

"I like hosting," he said, "because it's the only job in show business that means anything to me. By that, I mean it's a job that was there when I started in show business and it's still there—it's like stepping into a long-running play."

When Josef Woodard interviewed Leno for the *Santa Barbara News-Press,* he said:

"Television seems a natural medium for you. You're good at hosting the 'Tonight Show,' which you can't say for a lot of people who sit in that interviewer's hot seat."

Leno responded with a smile. "It's because I'm not a very interesting person myself, and I don't have any interest in show business. So I'm more interested in what other people have to say. I'm not doing any earth-shattering projects and I don't plan to. I really don't enjoy talking about myself. I'm not one of those 'here's my needs' people."

Another night Leno was talking to Donna Mills, who had just been voted an important honor. She was cited as one of the ten sexiest women in America. Donna acted flustered when the fact was brought up. "I don't know what *that* means."

Leno stared at her. He could see the false modesty just popping out all over her. The obvious thing might be to compliment her on her sexiness, but Leno's mind does not work that way.

"Take a guess," he said. "What do you *think* it means?"

To Leno it meant one thing and one thing only: the publicist she had hired to get her name out there in the public for her work on "Knots Landing" was just doing his job.

But he does not always get his laughs by sizzling his

guests. One night Shelley Winters was on the show and the conversation turned to sex and age. The discussion had not reached any conclusion on the age at which a person might have to give up the pleasures of sex. Instead of pontificating in any way, Leno simply looked over off-camera at the executive producer of the show—Fred de Cordova—and said:

"Fred?"

The audience absolutely broke up. Even septuagenarian de Cordova was laughing.

11

Support Team

WHILE JAY LENO was performing once a week as permanent guest host on the "Tonight Show," waiting patiently for May 22, 1992, he was quietly and effectively performing a number of behind-the-scenes chores that might be referred to as housekeeping duties—duties that would in the long run establish him as a star of late-night television.

No performer can be any better than those with whom he surrounds himself. Leno had enough sense from the beginning to realize that he would be no exception to this inexorable rule of professional virtuosity. The success of the show would depend completely on him.

And so as he continued to woo his national audience in his once-a-week television appearances and his local audiences all over the country in his road appearances, he was assembling a formidable work force to help propel him to the top and to keep him there.

From the moment he had entertained the idea of *being* the "Tonight Show," Leno knew that he had always acted on his own—no props, no gimmicks, no entourage, no stooge. And quite naturally he never considered using an Ed Mc-Mahon (second banana) or Doc Severinsen (third banana) to help bolster his image. His image would stand—or fall—on its own. He would do his opening monologue alone.

There were other concomitant considerations though. The format of the "Tonight Show" demanded a musical director, and Leno and his advisers fretted the most over the selection of this key player. In the end the choice turned out to be a somewhat daring sociological statement made by the cautiously and consummately politically correct Jay Leno.

Back in 1962, when Johnny Carson had taken over the "Tonight Show," he found himself with a similar decision to make regarding the leader of the studio orchestra. Clark Terry and Doc Severinsen sat right next to one another in the band that backed up Jack Paar. Terry was a well-known black trumpeter. Letters in support of Terry appeared at NBC, from viewers who wanted to see him leading the band under Carson's regime.

Terry later said, "It leaked out that [such a choice for leader] would kill the 'Tonight Show' in the Southern markets." Naturally, "they couldn't come out and *say* that. But there was a little hanky-panky about it."

In the end, Carson and NBC selected Doc Severinsen.

In 1991, history seemed to be about to repeat itself. An up-and-coming black jazz saxophonist termed by some a "cornerstone of the American jazz renaissance"—Branford Marsalis—had begun to make a name for himself in the decade he had been playing on the road. Starting out in New Orleans, he had joined his brother Wynton's jazz quintet.

Soon he was backing up pop star Sting, playing while Sting danced, and then he even appeared in movies by Spike Lee and Danny DeVito. His is featured on albums with such musicians as Dizzy Gillespie and Public Enemy and has made six of his own—most recently "The Beautyful Ones Are Not Yet Born."

Bobby Colomby, a drummer for Blood, Sweat & Tears, suggested Marsalis to Jay Leno, and Leno agreed to speak to

NBC about him. When Marsalis got the phone call from his manager, telling Marsalis that Jay Leno, who was going to *be* the "Tonight Show" after Carson's retirement, had asked for him to lead the studio orchestra, Marsalis laughed at the news.

"I said no," he recalled with a grin. "I didn't even have to think about it."

Quite probably he had heard the original scenario on the Doc Severinsen scam and did not want to play the sockee in a racist skirmish like the one that had done in Terry.

Marsalis was once again called, his manager informing him that the offer—quite definitely a solid one—had been made again. Would Marsalis replace Doc Severinsen as the musical director of the "Tonight Show"?

The question, to Marsalis, was not a simple one. Some elements of a studio leader's job bothered him. The best part of a creative artist's life was the ability to pull up stakes and go whenever the inclination presented itself. And yet, of course, a rootless existence was a precarious one. . . .

After refusal number two, Marsalis went and told his drummer and bassist what had happened so that they could share with him the full flavor of the jest.

Marsalis was brought up short by their reactions.

"They said we should do it!" Marsalis blinked his eyes.

Why not? they wondered.

"Hell no!" snapped Marsalis, shocked at their line of thinking.

But then *he* began pondering. And the more he thought about it, the more sense it made. And the more sense it made, the more he began making plans for the future. In the end, after some negotiating—and the negotiations were tough and formal at that—the deal was cut and the news was released for public consumption.

On December 12, 1991, it was thus made official. Branford Marsalis, at the age of thirty-one, would replace Doc

Severinsen—and to a certain extent, Ed McMahon as well. Since, indeed, Severinsen and McMahon were second and third bananas to Johnny Carson's top banana.

Certain diehards expressed themselves as "concerned" about Marsalis's professional integrity. His more hard-nosed fans were wondering whether or not he was "selling out his art," in their with-it terminology.

To this concern Marsalis had a musician's typical rejoinder. For twelve years he had traveled the road, existing in bone-grinding exhaustion during the gigs and worrying about ever working again when the gigs were done.

"If this is what art is," Marsalis said, referring to the incessant travel routine, "then, fuck art."

The "Tonight" deal was almost too good to be true, he decided. "We'll always be in the same city," he said. "I'll wake up in the same bed—first of all, I'll know the *size* of my bed every day. I can get whatever *food* I want when I want it.

"I won't have to take shit from nobody. I won't even have to deal with unscrupulous promoters. I won't have to hear from airlines telling us our cargo is too heavy and we have to send it freight—with a gig due in five hours."

Marsalis chuckled.

"This is a level of stability that I've never had since I left my parents' house in 1979. This is a good business move and a good personal move for me."

Nevertheless, some of his close musical associates wondered if it might not dull his creative edge.

"I don't know," Marsalis admitted to them. "That's the exciting part about it."

But Marsalis knew that his art would never leave him, since he had every intention of continuing to practice it as he had always done.

"We have to believe in our music enough and be dedicated enough to take the extra step and spend most of our free nights playing in clubs," he said. "We have to do that or we will wind up on the same musical level as the previous band, as our 'Tonight Show' predecessors.

"The onus is on the person that does the job: is it more important to live in the lap of luxury and live a life of ease—which is definitely possible doing a show like this—or will you stay dedicated to the music?"

Marsalis announced that the band would include Bob Hurst, bassist, and Jeff Watts, drummer—probably the most accomplished rhythm section of his generation, according to jazz aficionados. Also included would be Kevin Eubanks, guitarist, and Matt Finders and Sal Marquez, both horn men, and a percussionist and a pianist who were at that time still undecided.

Marsalis and Jay Leno had discussed the type of music that would predominate, for Leno had a definite concept of the kind of thing he wanted.

"As for the music," he told Marsalis, "I like the idea of an orchestra like the one we have now. You don't want to do the same as other shows, like David Letterman, who has a rock band. People really like the 'Tonight Show' orchestra."

Marsalis understood perfectly. He liked a hint of jazz in his music—but jazz had come to have such a wide definition that many different types of pop music were *called* jazz even if they might not be specifically such.

However, he indicated that he would stay away from the complex, abstract music that he and Watts and Hurst had been playing in their late 1991 concerts.

Marsalis was quick to admit that he was not like his brother Wynton, who wanted to bring jazz to the people. "You can't bring anything to an audience on their terms," he said.

Comparing his own concepts with those of the studio orchestra backing up the Arsenio Hall show, Marsalis pointed out an interesting difference:

"Jay Leno's humor is very political, very adult-oriented.

Arsenio's just a talk-show host and the comedian of the beautiful people. So everything that's pop and hip and in— Arsenio's right on the pulse of that."

In 1980, Marsalis played in Clark Terry's band. One of the first people he called when he had decided to take the "Tonight Show" job was Terry. "I told him he'd better go and grab that opportunity," Terry said.

The significance of the change in audience reaction did not escape Marsalis. About Jay Leno's selection of him, Marsalis said:

"It's an important statement, I think. To have some black people on the whitest show in America" was really something.

One of Jay Leno's first orders to Marsalis concerned the theme song of the "Tonight Show." It had been written for Johnny Carson by none other than famed singing star Paul Anka.

"It's got to go," Leno told Marsalis. "We get something new. It's like hearing 'Thanks for the Memory' and having everyone say, 'So, where's Bob Hope?'" Marsalis agreed with Leno.

Perhaps even more important to the ultimate success or failure of the "Tonight Show" was the selection of its producer—the person with whom Jay Leno would have to work the most effectively and the most closely.

Fred de Cordova, who had been the show's producer all during Carson's stint, along with director Peter Lassally, his associate, would be leaving the show along with Carson. Leno had a replacement in mind.

One night in 1975, when Jay Leno was newly arrived in Los Angeles and happened to be sleeping overnight in his car, a woman came to the Comedy Store to watch his act. Her name then was Helen Gorman. She was an agent who represented writers and producers in television. She liked Leno and his routine enough to meet him personally the next day.

The interest was reciprocated by Leno. He signed on as her client then and there.

It was Gorman who sent Leno on the road all over the country, blocking out his travel schedules, booking his appearances, and helping him to develop his career.

She was the one—now Helen Gorman Kushnick—who followed NBC executives around talking up Jay Leno and finally drew up the contract that put him in the driver's seat at the helm of the "Tonight Show."

In the negotiations that surrounded Jay Leno's starring on the "Tonight Show," it was decided that she would take over from Fred de Cordova as executive producer.

Helen Gorman Kushnick would now be part and parcel of the talent she had nurtured through some of the trying and insubstantial years of Leno's long, arduous, and slow-building career.

Helen Gorman was going out with Jerry Kushnick, a lawyer, when she became Jay Leno's agent. When Kushnick and she married in 1979, they formed a management firm—a company that handled not only Jay Leno, but comedians Jimmie Walker, David Letterman, Elayne Boosler, and Debbie Allen as well.

In 1980 Helen Kushnick gave birth to twins, Sara and Sam, both prematurely. At Cedars-Sinai Medical Center, Sam and Sara were given blood transfusions as was customary with preemies.

At the age of two and a half, Sam caught a bad cold one day. It never went away. But the physicians told the Kushnicks not to worry. However, one day Sam became very ill and turned blue. A frightened Helen Kushnick had him rushed to Cedars. There, nothing could be done for him. He survived for nineteen days, but then died.

The truth came out. The blood that Sam had received by transfusion was tainted with the HIV virus, the virus responsible for AIDS.

Leno later told the story of what had faced the Kushnicks in those early days of the AIDS epidemic when no one really knew much about it and it was treated like some kind of dreaded secret.

"Sam was like the fourth child in Los Angeles to have AIDS. Or at least the fourth one that people knew about. It was like the flip side of winning the one hundred million dollar California lottery, a one-in-a-million chance. It was a great tragedy."

That was the beginning of many tragic situations for the Kushnicks. In 1989, six years after Sam's death, Jerry Kushnick developed colon cancer and died. As if that were not enough, in 1991, Helen Kushnick underwent a mastectomy, with the breast cancer finally diagnosed as in remission.

"We've been through a lot together," Helen Kushnick acknowledged. "And Jay's been incredibly supportive [of us]. He told Jerry before he died that if anything ever happened to Jerry, Jay would be there for Sam's twin, Sara. And both he and Mavis *have* been there."

It was through Jay Leno's support that Helen Kushnick landed the plum of a job as executive producer of the "Tonight Show."

Even so, before Jerry's death the Kushnicks were doing something about AIDS and its insidious effect even on people not in the groups at high risk for developing the disease.

At first, of course, the doctors at the hospital said they did not know what made Sam sick, or what caused him to die. It was days later that they finally admitted it was AIDS.

AIDS at the time was no more than a dark whisper echoing on the fringes of society. When the word about Sam's death by AIDS got out, his twin sister Sara's preschool, Temple Emanuel of Beverly Hills, sent a representative to Cedars-Sinai Medical Center the day after Sam died to inform the Kushnicks that Sara, his sister, would not be allowed to return to Temple Emanuel.

Jay Leno was sympathetic to the Kushnicks' personal problems.

He said, "Let's put my career on hold. I'll work the Improv instead of two weeks in Las Vegas. That's fine. Come back when you're ready. Your family comes first."

But Helen Kushnick wanted to do it her way. That is, to continue Leno's bookings. After Sam's death, the Kushnicks filed suit against Cedars-Sinai for not telling them about the tainted blood supply. The case was thrown out of court. ABC-TV's "20/20" told their story, and largely on the strength of that publicity, the Kushnicks established the Samuel Jared Kushnick Foundation to raise money for social services, research, and community-based programs to fight pediatric AIDS.

"We're paying now for not attacking the disease in 1981," Helen Kushnick said recently. "We've wasted ten years."

Grants for the Samuel Jared Kushnick Foundation are overseen by AIDS researchers Dr. Arthur Ammann of San Francisco and Dr. Geneva Woodruff of Boston. Ammann said recently that blood-transfusion AIDS deaths have become a rarity now. Most children with AIDS are born with it.

"I told Jerry before he died that he and Helen should really feel good, that they kept many children alive," Ammann said. "Without their pushing for more rigid blood screening, the cleaning of the blood supplies might have been delayed for another year.

"What's really amazing about Helen is that with all the trauma she's been through, she still has the time to be concerned about others. She is very direct and she speaks her mind. You don't always agree with her, but you know exactly where she stands."

That ingrained toughness came in handy in Helen Kushnick's role as Jay Leno's manager. She acted the bad cop to Leno's good cop. Besides booking his appearances and overseeing his career, she was the one who said no to the many requests for endorsements, appearances, and interviews. Sometimes, of course, she would say yes. She also scheduled Leno's guests for his once-a-week "Tonight Show" spot in 1991–92.

"Everything is coming together," she said recently, even if she might have been wondering what else could possibly happen to her. She was mostly concerned about bringing up her daughter, Sara, a blue-ribbon-winning horseback rider. Right after her twin brother's death, Sara suffered through terrible torments, taunted by children who couldn't play with her because of the disease that had killed her brother.

"It has made her a lot more sympathetic to people and sensitive to not hurting someone's feelings," Helen Kushnick said.

"Jerry was the great love of my life," she went on, pointing out that she has never dated anyone since his death. "I don't need the complications of dating. I've got the 'Tonight Show,' and a daughter to raise.

"I have the second-best job in television," she said. "Jay's got the best."

It was largely through trying to help the Kushnicks do something about AIDS that Jay Leno serendipitously became a professional author. At least he got his byline on three books published by Warner paperbacks.

The books were titled *Headlines, More Headlines,* and *Headlines III: Not the Movie, Still the Book.* Although he was listed as "author," he was actually an "editor" or "compiler."

The books grew out of a comedy routine Leno developed on the "Tonight Show" when he was appearing as guest host. He worked out a gag routine in which he would read aloud a real headline from a newspaper, holding it up for the audience to see, and then joking about it—rolling his eyes or grimacing or pulling some kind of funny face with his rubbery features.

Of course, the headline had to be obviously dumb—that is, a non sequitur, a nonsensical statement, or an obvious blooper of one kind or another.

In a way, it was an updated version of those 1930s *New Yorker* bloopers with comments added. In Leno's version, however, he simply made the proper face, then added a gag line to give an amusing double entendre to the somewhat puzzling headline itself.

The top blurb on the cover of the first book explained the content:

"As featured on the 'Tonight Show,'" the blurb says, and then the title, *Headlines*, follows. Leno's smiling face appears beside a clipped headline reading: "Dead Man Told: Get Back to Work."

Below that a subtitle reads: "Real but Ridiculous Samplings from America's Newspapers: Compiled by Jay Leno."

One typical sampling of the headlines inside reads:

Unemployment Not Working, Critics Say

Another reads:

Gas Chamber Executions May Be Health Hazard

Here's one with Leno's comment. Headline: "Researchers Call Murder a Threat to Public Health." Comment: "How long did this study take? Do you think it was more than ten minutes?" Leno's face, printed beside the caption, expresses some bafflement.

Or here's one:

Death in the Ring:
Most Boxers Are Not the Same Afterward

Leno's comment: "Yeah, I hear some of them are actually smarter."

Skiing Season Opens in Iran

the headline reads, about which Leno comments: "When I think of a skiing vacation, I think of three places: Vail . . . Aspen . . . Tehran."

Once the viewers caught on to the format, they began to send in clippings from their local papers to the "Tonight Show." Leno always avoided using headlines from the supermarket tabloids because the humorous double entendres in them were of course deliberate plays on words. He tried to select headlines from small-town papers and other straight-arrow publications.

White Flower Two-Day Sale—Friday Only

Huh?

Leno's response to the headline "Criminal Groups Infiltrating Pot Farms" was, "Criminal groups involved with drugs? Is *nothing* sacred?"

Actually, Leno did very little writing for these books. Most of the headlines speak for themselves. One can only speculate on the size of his advance from Warner paperbacks.

Leno kept none of the money made on the sale of the books. The royalties all went—and now go—to the Samuel Jared Kushnick Foundation to help children with AIDS. The first two books had earned more than $400,000 before the third one was published.

Actually author Jay Leno feels uncomfortable about publicity on any work he does for charity, believing that "good work should be done anonymously."

His books unfortunately failed to earn overwhelming critical acclaim, even though they sold and continue to sell quite well.

One critic sniffed: "Hey, why should the money go to charity? They're charity laughs."

"The money from the books goes directly to the kids,"

Leno pointed out. "They're lying in the hospitals and feeling terrible. They want to watch TV and all that's on is 'General Hospital.' So we get them VCRs and Disney tapes, so at least they can find something to watch. And that just feels great."

To round out her appointments to carry the "Tonight Show" when Jay Leno would take over on May 25, 1992, Helen Kushnick selected Ellen Brown to direct the show. Brown had been working with Leno ever since he had started his "Tonight Show" guest-hostings.

Late in January 1992, Kushnick and Leno auditioned a number of announcers to do the voice-overs and the off-camera work on the upcoming show. The man who won the final bid was Edd Hall, who had worked for the Fox Broadcasting series "Married . . . with Children" and "Get a Life" and who had served as a graphic designer for "Late Night with David Letterman." In 1979 he had been a page for "Saturday Night Live." Later he worked for Home Box Office, Showtime, and the Learning Channel.

Edd Hall claimed that he had added the second *d* to his name for the sake of "pizzazz." It was said that his audition tape contained samples of Hall's extensive repertoire of more than 150 voices—voices he used on "Married" and "Letterman."

"I don't mind behind-the-camera," Hall told *People* magazine. "I am basically a lazy guy." When he was fourteen years old, Hall had become a teenage disc jockey in Corning, New York, where he grew up.

According to Hall's wife, Liza Forster, a talent coordinator, her husband and Leno seem to have parallel comedic talents, judging from a scene she saw shortly after Hall was selected as Leno's announcer.

It was at the wedding of a mutual friend. "Jay was tormenting Edd by sticking wedding flowers in his ears," Forster said.

"There are advantages to being just a voice and not a face

on television," Hall joked. "I can go to Bagel Nosh and not be recognized."

Hall's stepfather, Bill Hall, said that Hall's apparent modesty is a smoke screen. "When he gave us his new phone number, he told us not to release it to anyone—the words of a true rising star."

12

On the Fringes

J AY LENO'S CLIMB to the big time as host of the number one national nighttime television talk show was hardly a straight-arrow ascent. During that climb he frequently rested along the way on side roads that seemed attractive—or necessary—to him at the time.

For example, he occasionally took a chance at guest shots on several of television's more popular sitcoms—appearing in light comedy roles that seemed right for him—including roles on "Laverne & Shirley" and "One Day at a Time."

Both series, of course, are history today.

"Laverne & Shirley," which aired for a long run of eight years from 1976 through 1983, starred Penny Marshall and Cindy Williams. In effect, it was a kind of flashback to the light comedy dramas of the late 1930s spun off the popularity of the prototypical Broadway hit comedy, *My Sister Eileen.* The most popular of these clones was "My Friend Irma," which played to modest acclaim on radio and TV.

Like its models, "Laverne & Shirley" concerned two working-class women, one sharp, quick, and defensive (Laverne) and the other trusting, naive, and a born victim (Shirley). The class milieu was definitely blue collar; the characters supposedly worked in a brewery on the bottle-cap assembly line. No one ever saw the shop; all the action took place in their apartment. Leno's perfect built-in blue-collar persona worked effectively for his bit part in this series.

In the episode, he played Laverne's "evil" boyfriend. "I was mean to Laverne," he explained. "At the end of the show, I dumped her."

A few days after that, Leno was out shopping, and a woman came up to him and accosted him loudly.

"This lady starts yelling at me," Leno said, "because I was mean to Laverne."

A bit shaken, Leno tried to explain: "Ma'am, it's the *character* I played. Really—I'm a *friend* of Penny's."

The woman refused to believe it and stalked off mumbling to herself, convinced that Leno was a monster. It was one of his first encounters with an aggrieved fan who *believed* the "baddie" role he was playing.

"One Day at a Time" aired concurrently with "Laverne & Shirley," from 1975 through 1984, and starred Bonnie Franklin, Mackenzie Phillips, and Valerie Bertinelli—a divorced mother and her two teenage daughters trying to make their way amidst a myriad of obstacles and distractions dreamed up by imaginative scriptwriters.

This was yet another version of *My Sister Eileen,* featuring, in addition to the three leads, their building super and their various boyfriends and associates. Again, the milieu was definitely working class. Leno fit in perfectly.

None of his guest spots lit up the sky. Leno continued his wide-ranging road trips with these infrequent side excursions. In the end, it appeared that Leno had always known what was best for Leno.

Finally, when Leno was invited to serve as guest host on the "Tonight Show" in 1986, he became more than just a one-dimensional comedian. He was now also an interviewer and stand-up comic for the country's most-viewed late-night talk show.

He and his agent-manager were finally able to convince NBC-TV that his fifteen years as a stand-up comic had made him a viable candidate for a comedy special of some kind. He was signed to develop three late-night specials for 1986—and perhaps work on a comedy series to star himself—beginning perhaps in 1987.

His gigs on "Late Night with David Letterman," "Saturday Night Live," and "Friday Night Videos" continued during that time, along with his spate of guest-host gigs on the Carson show.

The early months of 1986 had Leno producing a comedy special for Home Box Office, the big cable channel. The show was an amalgam of clips from his regular stand-up routines during a road visit to Chicago along with a series of special comedy sketches filmed at sites around the Windy City. The clips and sketches were then spliced together, edited, and smoothed up for showing on the cable channel.

The resulting "comedy special" was an unqualified success. The two separate types of comedy—ad-lib and prepared—supported one another, providing Leno with what turned out to be a perfect showcase for his special talents.

It was largely because of this effort that NBC was persuaded Leno could handle his own special. What he finally decided to do was to produce a long, ninety-minute show in the same kind of loose format: a series of live acts interspersed with location sketches of an ad-lib nature. It would be a combination of Leno onstage and Leno at large.

He was happy with the concept. The Chicago HBO show had proved the perfect format for his talents. He preferred to be himself rather than someone else. He was a personality, not an actor. Why not be just Jay Leno?

"I get to play myself," he said happily in discussing his special. "It's not like I'm playing a wacky neighbor or something, where you think, 'Oh, boy, it's gonna be embarrassing if it's not good.'"

NBC arranged for the special to be filmed on location in Philadelphia. The theater was not a theater at all, but an enormous warehouse called Pier 12—a kind of cavernous soundstage built beneath a bridge—where the audience would sit around to watch both the acts as they occurred on a central stage and the pretaped spots projected on a huge screen behind it.

Explaining why he opted to use this rather strange format in his first network TV special, Leno admitted, "I didn't want to start right in with a TV show per se. It's the same attitude I have in the clubs. Let me try something a couple of times, to see if it works."

He wanted to concentrate strictly on comedy. "What we're trying to do, more or less, is bring back variety. The only place you see comedians nowadays on TV is the 'Tonight Show' or the Letterman show. That's it. When I was a kid, if you wanted to see comedians or dancers or even singers, you had Ed Sullivan, the 'Dean Martin Show,' the 'Glen Campbell Goodtime Hour,' Flip Wilson. . . .

"There are a lot more comedians around today, but they're not on TV. Cable television has been a tremendous help. I think cable helped get more interest in all the comedians."

Yet Leno was somewhat ambivalent about a "special." A composed, thought-out *structured* project was *different* from a guest spot or a hosting job. Leno confessed that rehearsed, prewritten material was simply not *natural* for him.

"I would much rather ad-lib than rehearse something. For a special like this, you write the sketch; then you show it to someone; and then you make changes and you rehearse it; and then you block it and edit it." Leno sighed. "I would rather say, 'Let's just do it.'"

But that was not the way it was with a special.

"With 'Tonight,' I think up jokes that afternoon and I do them that night. You go on instinct, and when you go on instinct, the adrenaline is there. Doing a sketch eight times, backwards and forwards, is just not the same thing. Dealing with all the details can make you nutty."

For example:

"I said I wanted one of the sets to look just like a house. Then someone came up to me and said, 'Jay, how big do you want the doorway?'

"'Huh?'

"'How big do you want the doorway? Forty-one inches or forty-six inches?'

"'I don't know. How wide's a doorway? Just put it in.'"

Leno: "The thing people forget about TV, really, is that no one cares. It kills me to see these guys who've been hanging around show business forever, and now they're telling me, 'Hey, got my own show!'

"It's not that big a deal. I was once offered one of those spots—a late-night deal on ABC-TV. I told them the show I wanted to do, the Letterman show, was already on. So when NBC started talking about *this* variety show, it got my interest."

He remembered two ways he used to watch a variety show on television. "You sat through the music to get to the comedy, or you sat through the comedy to get to the music. When the Beatles were on the Ed Sullivan show in 1964, I was the only kid in America waiting for Alan King to come on with jokes about the insurance company."

As things progressed, Leno grew less and less sanguine about the special he was working on. After all, there were limitations to television. He was a comedian, no matter what medium he played on: live stage, film, television. He could not figure out how to cope with some of the difficulties that came up.

In spite of the problems he began to meet as his work went ahead, Leno planned his moves in meticulous detail. He knew that one of the main reasons for his success on television were his appearances on David Letterman's show. Thus Letterman was a special link. NBC agreed to let him use Letterman, and so Letterman was signed on, along with Vanna White of "Wheel of Fortune" and Doug Llewelyn of "People's Court."

The main plot gimmick turned on the popularity of a phenomenon then beginning to excite the American people all over the country: the so-called murder weekend. You know: assemble a lot of guests at a hotel or resort, have actors mix with the guests, cause one of them—or more—to be murdered, and ring in an actor-detective to solve the crime, with the guests helping out.

The victim in this one, of course, was—who else?— David Letterman. And so after a too-brief appearance at the start of the show, there is a sudden flash of light, and the set goes to black. When the lights come on again, Letterman is lying in a heap on the floor. He has been shot dead. Soon some attendants arrive with a gurney and wheel him off to oblivion.

Who shot David Letterman?

And that is where Vanna White comes in. She arranges the clues that are spotted on a pegboard—a parody of the big letter chart she uses for "Wheel."

Of course, as the drama continues, spots are inserted— short takes of Jay Leno on the streets of Philadelphia chatting with people and discussing such profound subjects as the reason Dick Clark moved "American Bandstand" out of Philadelphia twenty years ago. In this Q and A, Leno becomes an interrogator in the "60 Minutes" fashion, visiting the headquarters of "American Bandstand," now deserted, for an in-depth study of "the enigma of Dick Clark."

One sketch involves Doug Llewelyn, emcee of the "People's Court," who participates in a minidrama about a real courtroom that tries to adopt "People's Court" tactics to adjudicate cases.

However good all this looked on paper, on the air the special simply did not pan out. The critics—*and* the public—pounced on it immediately.

Lee Margulies of the *Los Angeles Times* started his critique in this daunting manner: "'Remember,' cohost Lu Leonard says at the outset of Jay Leno's first network special tonight, 'if you don't like this one, there won't be any more!'

"That's called leading with your chin. Leno's got a formidable one, which is a good thing, because he lands on it in this ninety-minute substitute for 'Saturday Night Live.'"

Margulies eventually buried the show with these words: "'The Jay Leno Show,' in short, is the very thing it seeks to satirize: doltish television."

John J. O'Connor of the *New York Times* wrote: "The show is a clumpy mess." He did give accolades to Leno himself, pointing out that he was a fine comic, deftly taking on a wide range of subjects for satire. O'Connor felt it had been a mistake to tape the show at Philadelphia's Pier 12, the warehouse under the bridge. The essential humor seemed to be lost in the vastness of the hall, with many of the live audience unable to tell what was going on much of the time.

The mood at Pier 12 at the end of the special had "gone rather sullen," he wrote.

He also criticized the focus of the show—pointing out that the best of the material seemed to flash past so quickly that the audience had no time to respond. About the mystery surrounding the "death" of Letterman, O'Connor wrote: "'Tain't funny, McGee."

Nevertheless, he liked Leno's stand-up skit about a flight on a chartered plane, a kind of "flying slave ship" on which the movie shown was *Eraserhead.* Leno's comment about the flight was that when this kind of plane goes down, "you only hear about it on cable television."

According to Tom Shales of the *Washington Post,* "Leno ends up seeming like just another ruthless comedy jerk."

Calling the show "feeble," he said that it "doesn't ever quite get to its feet, much less stand up." In sum, "it all seems a little too desperate. And insufficiently hilarious."

The somewhat obvious failure of his initial television network special brought Jay Leno up short. He had thought the format adopted for the Chicago cable special adequate for late-night television: obviously he had been wrong. The sketches did not seem to come off, either. Perhaps he needed to train himself a little more fully in a theatrical sense.

At the time of the airing of the Philadelphia special, Leno admitted:

"I wasn't real happy with it. It didn't come out the way I wanted, but I guess people always say that."

It was time to take a breather and look around a bit. While Leno was in this mood of "looking around," he was reading a number of motion picture scripts sent to his agent-manager by various producers. Leno was not new to film. He had appeared in at least four pictures.

Perhaps he needed this kind of broadening. He had never really *liked* being considered an actor. He had always wanted to be *himself,* playing the comic that he was. And yet it was obvious that there were dramatic flaws in his first special. Maybe he could learn something from film if he tried it again.

He often shuddered when he looked back on his "film career." It is one subject that he does not like to joke about. "Film career? I never had one," he admitted tersely. "I made a few movies that didn't do very well. Besides, good reviews aren't enough for a film career. Either a movie makes money or it doesn't. It's like a joke. Either it's funny or it's not. If people like it, it's a good movie. If they don't like it, then you get into that gray area. They didn't understand it. Yeah, fine. Comedy clubs are filled with comics who are misunderstood."

Whenever he was asked if he intended to pursue his acting career in films, Leno would turn defensive. "I don't know. If Sidney Lumet or one of those terrific directors said, 'Gee, I think you'd be good for this,' I guess I would do it. It's not like people are offering me *Godfather III*. What they come to me with is more like *Hamburger: the Movie, Part II*."

About the four films he *did* make:

In 1977 he played a very small part in a picture titled *Fun With Dick and Jane*. This was a Jane Fonda movie, directed by Ted Kotcheff. "Jane" was Jane Fonda, and "Dick" was George Segal. Ed McMahon also had a role in the picture, along with Allan Miller and John Dehner.

In the story "Dick" lost his job, and he and his wife, "Jane," had to cope with the lack of income. They turned to crime, where everything suddenly fell apart for them. So did the picture, which soon became fragmented and hard to follow.

Leno called his appearance in the picture a "don't-blink-your-eyes walk-on."

Then Leno was hired for a part in a 1978 movie titled *American Hot Wax*. This was a much more successful picture, directed by Floyd Mutrux. The story was "based on fact"— what facts weren't particularly evident—but it purported to be taken from the life of the famous disc jockey Alan Freed. Tim McIntire played Freed, with Fran Drescher, John Lehne, Laraine Newman, Jeff Altman, Chuck Berry, Jerry Lee Lewis, and Screamin' Jay Hawkins—along with Jay Leno—making up the balance of the cast.

Leno played the role of a chauffeur with just the proper touch of reserve and panache. In fact, he was listed in the cast of the picture. He had not been listed in *Fun With Dick and Jane*. He felt it might at least be a step upward in his film career.

His next role was as the son of a mafioso in *Silver Bears*, a motion picture version of Paul Erdman's novel scripted by Peter Stone. Directed by Ivan Passer, the film starred Michael

Caine, Cybill Shepherd, Louis Jourdan, Martin Balsam, Stephane Audran, Tommy Smothers, David Warner, Charles Gray, and Jay Leno. Quite a satisfactory cast!

The story was of course about very high-level money manipulation in the international silver market. Leno looked just right for the part he played.

His next film was titled *Americathon*. Harvey Korman and John Ritter were the stars, along with Nancy Morgan. The 1979 picture was directed by Neil Israel. A large cast including such oddities as Chief Dan George, Tommy Lasorda, Meat Loaf, and Howard Hesseman—and narrated voice-over by George Carlin—should have insured a good picture.

Leno played a prize-fighter. The premise was a good one: in 1988, America was forced to hold a telethon in order to raise enough money to save itself from bankruptcy. The bad news was that in his role Leno had to box with an old lady who was supposed to be his mother!

The film was, sadly, a bomb.

Leno was beginning to wonder if film held anything for him. He could still do his nightly gigs. He could still travel around the country. He could still guest-host on the "Tonight Show." What was he fooling around in film for?

And yet. . . .

Among the scripts that came to hand at the time was one titled *Collision Course*. It was a "culture-clash" story about a Japanese police detective and a Detroit police detective teamed up inadvertently to solve the murder of a Japanese businessman in Detroit. Pat Morita, the famed *Karate Kid* mentor, had already been signed on as the Japanese lead.

"When I read the *Collision Course* script," Leno said, "I was so impressed with it and the chance to work with Pat Morita that I met with Brandon Tartikoff [NBC entertainment president], who graciously permitted me to postpone my commitment to NBC for this television season."

And then began the long negotiations for a three-picture

contract with Dino De Laurentiis. To make the contract legal, certain details had to be excluded from Leno's three-special contract with NBC. Everything was eventually ironed out, and Leno finally went to work on the picture.

That meant getting to Detroit for the early location shots. Leno didn't mind the grind of memorizing lines and of the retakes and so on. But he was not exclusively a motion picture actor and had to find time for his gigs and hosting jobs.

"It was a killer, juggling all that stuff. Movies aren't *fun* to make. I'd be on the set and then have to be onstage somewhere at nine-thirty, then have to get back to the location [in Detroit] by two in the morning so I could be on the set at six A.M. again. That was a little wacky. I don't think I'll do it again. But I won't give up stand-up to do movies. Stand-up is what I like best."

During the filming of the movie, Leno was visited by numerous reporters for interviews, among them *Chicago Tribune* film critic Gene Siskel.

"I had been offered other lead roles before this one," Leno said. "Usually the offer was for some generic comedy like *Hot Dog: The Movie* or *Hamburger: The Movie* or *Pizza Shop: The Movie.*"

Leno shrugged. "I didn't want to do anything like that. I wanted to do a movie about a real guy in a real situation. My attitude about myself is that I'm sort of average looking. Not too tall, not too short. Not in good shape, not in bad shape. Most of my comedy comes from my going places and being treated rudely or buying a product that's mislabeled.

"In other words, I like being the foil and having things happen to me and around me. In this movie I've been busy giving jokes written for my character to the other actors."

The big problem, as Leno saw it, was that most comics moving from comedy to film found themselves playing characters that were cornier onscreen than off.

"I think an exception was Rodney Dangerfield in *Back to*

School," Leno observed. "What I liked about it is that he didn't strictly play the guy he plays in his stand-up. He was just a guy. And his son loved him. And he loved his son. And the humor grew out of that. I'm so tired of films where the comedy is all insults, where you try to get a laugh calling someone a name."

Leno thought a minute.

"So much of comedy is negative. 'My wife's a pain; my kid's a jerk; my old man's a . . .' I'm not saying *my* approach is right and theirs is wrong; it's just my preference. Whether on stage or on film, I prefer comedy that makes you feel good rather than has you come out thinking, 'Yeah, I guess the world really does suck.'"

He had his own ideas about the picture he was making.

"Actually, *Collision Course* wasn't written strictly as a comedy. It's a cop picture. Pat plays a Japanese detective who comes from Tokyo to investigate the theft of some plans for a special turbocharger. I play Tony Costas, a Detroit cop investigating a murder in a junkyard. Since a Japanese man was killed in the junkyard, and Pat is snooping around there, I wind up chasing him for the first part of the film."

Making the picture, Leno pointed out, was a decided change from constructing a stand-up routine.

"It's strange for me to take six months to tell a joke rather than just tell it. We sit around, the cast and I, with the director [Lewis Teague, *The Jewel of the Nile*] and the writers, and we keep asking ourselves, 'Is this funny? Is this funny? Is this funny?'

"Earlier today, for example, I thought of a joke I considered pretty good. In the scene Pat and I are together. We confront the bad guys, about six of them, in a warehouse. Pat knocks over some shelving to divert everybody. I grab one of the bad guys."

The script calls for Leno to say, "You better let us go or we will kill your friend."

To which one of the bad guys says, "Friend?" And instantly blows him away!

Leno and Morita have to duck down out of sight to get away from the mob men.

"The crew laughed," Leno said. "We put it in. That's the way I work." The crew became Leno's test audience.

"It's hard to foretell the proper public reaction," Leno admitted. "That's why we shoot some scenes two ways. Just for protection. We can decide later in the editing [which one plays]. Also, we're not altering the basic structure of the scenes based on the crew; we're just testing some jokes. You can like working with an audience, but basically you still use your own instinct."

Leno chuckled. "Just the other day I came up with a joke that might be a bit much. I pull out a badge and say, 'Police!' and one of the bad guys pulls out his gun and says, 'Criminal!'" Leno winced. "Don't worry, we shot the scene without the gag, too."

Leno had a solid sense of his image on the screen. He made the writers change it when his and their concepts did not quite jibe.

"They had this scene at the beginning of the movie where I beat up this giant thug [played by the humongous Tex Cobb]. I said, 'No way. Let's have him beat me up. I mean, I look like a guy who would get beat up.'

"And that's about as deep as I get into acting. I'm not thinking of my character's motivation. It's more like Dean Martin playing Matt Helm. Actually, I'd rather think of myself more like James Garner, at least in my easygoing manner."

About making films in general, Leno said, "It's just another branch of [show] business. I'll try anything if people think I can be good at it."

He recognized the drawbacks of filming from the first, of course. "I'd honestly rather have the spontaneity of the audience instead of rehearsing something a dozen times, filming it, and then waiting a good six months to see if it works."

What was discouraging to him was that he did not have a live audience on which he could test the viability of his material.

"We more or less improvised and made up things as we went along. It's a little different working in front of a movie camera than doing a live show because you do your material, but you get no reaction. You do a funny joke, and the cameraman says, 'Gimme another shot of that, Bob.' And you say, 'Gee, didn't you hear the joke?'

"Did you ever see *The Jolson Story?* He's just staring at the camera and he says, *'Where are the people?'* That's what it's like."

Plus which, the film had directorial problems. John Guillermin was the original director, with Bob Clark taking over in the middle of production. But Clark didn't stay long. Soon Lewis Teague took over, and it was his name that finally wound up on the credits.

And from the directorial conflicts other problems seemed to spread out like the cracks in a ceiling.

By the time the picture was in the can, Leno was having second thoughts about making any pictures at all.

"Movies are not for me," he said emphatically. "It may be fun once the movie comes out, but there is no audience for a movie. You do it into space for a camera."

On the other hand—

"If the movie's a hit, I'm in good shape. . . . But if it's a bomb . . ."

In the end, the picture was made, the film edited, the release date scheduled—and then suddenly Dino De Laurentiis caught the disease of the 1990s—bankruptcy—and everything he had on film was shelved.

For Leno, all this—including the seemingly bizarre

nonending of the project—was just another example of show-biz *inceptus interruptus*. He was not bitter, he was simply philosophical, as he had always been.

And then suddenly in April 1992 the whole story of *Collision Course* turned around and began traveling in the opposite direction. HBO Video announced that it was releasing the 1987 motion picture on the home video market.

Backtracking to find out what happened, Leno observers discovered that when De Laurentiis went bankrupt, *Collision Course* ended up in the hands of Wells Fargo Bank.

Robert W. Cort, one of the film's producers, and president of Interscope Communications, said that the movie simply sat on the shelf at Wells Fargo. "We were never able to get it released." The bankers had inflated hopes for the film. They wanted to sell it at full price for theatrical release, but they could find no takers.

Leno was not necessarily thrilled at the prospect of his first starring role appearing on home videotape.

"They're just taking advantage of where Jay is now," said Helen Kushnick. Nor was his agent. "It's so obvious. We had nothing to do with the release of this movie now."

Of course, the tremendous publicity blitz unleashed to coincide with Leno's taking over as host of the "Tonight Show" could only help make the movie a success—even on the small screen.

According to Andy Marx in the *Los Angeles Times*, the promo material released with *Collision Course* stated that the film came "from the makers of *The Jewel of the Nile, Airplane!* and *Airplane II: The Sequel.* Lewis Teague, the third director, and the director of credit, did direct *Jewel*, but not the *Airplane!* movies. Cort worked on the *Airplane!* films, but had nothing to do with *Jewel*.

What did Leno think about all this sudden resurrection of *Collision* so close to the time of his debut on "Tonight"?

"I make my living on the road. This TV [and film] stuff is, like, extra. I know it sounds terribly snobby, but I'm just very happy doing what I'm doing."

Anyway, the reception some other films got always puzzled Leno. He was once discussing the movie *Blue Velvet*, David Lynch's dark psychosexual film.

"Mavis and I went to see it, and I said, 'Uh, yeah?' And my wife said, 'Oh, Jay, it was wonderful,' and she told me about it." Short pause. "I guess I liked it better after she told me about it."

He confessed how he felt when he went out to see *Americathon*, one of his earlier films.

"What a terrible movie!"

In fact, on viewing it he thought it was even worse than he had thought it was when he was making it.

American Hot Wax was a definite success, of course. The studio wanted to remake it as a film-for-television some years after it opened.

"I went over to the studio where they were going to film it and saw a note on the board," Leno said. "They were asking for actors to play the roles in the movie."

He tried to laugh at the note on his own role: "We need a Jay Leno type—but *better looking*"!

13

Cabbages and Presidents

WHETHER IT WAS THE USO or Jay Leno who initiated the comedian's visit to U.S. troops stationed in Saudi Arabia preparatory to the Persian Gulf War of 1991 matters little. It was the *idea* itself that counted. And so it was with bated breath that Chapman Cox, president of the World USO, announced early in September 1990 that Jay Leno would be making that all-important morale-building visit "sometime around Thanksgiving."

"We are incredibly excited about being able to send someone of Jay's caliber to represent Americans back home who deeply appreciate the sacrifices being made in the Persian Gulf," Cox said.

Kevin McCarthy, executive producer for the USO, echoed Cox's sentiments. "We're all seeing that the enemy the troops are fighting right now is boredom and loneliness." This was, of course, some months before the real shooting began. "Jay Leno will fix that. If the troops are still there at Thanksgiving, this will be a welcome break for them."

While Leno was volunteering his time and talent, the USO was paying for the trip by dipping into a $2-million USO Gulf Crisis Fund that had been set up for just such a

179

contingency. Other celebrity tours were scheduled to begin in the fall of 1990.

Leno immediately had his own comments about visiting the troops.

"It's going to be great," he exulted. "I mean, it's a *captive* audience. Where are they going to go—walk ten miles into the desert?"

He recalled his own draft experience in the Vietnam War.

"My draft number was two sixty-two. I wasn't called." He grinned. "My country hasn't asked me to do much, so if they ask me to go and entertain, I'll go."

Leno said that he would tell the troops his favorite jokes and get some new tropical material for them.

"Reserves, huh?" he said, ad-libbing a joke on the spot. "I bet Vice President Quayle won't be there. I guess he must have called his dad on that one."

Leno promised not to do any Arab-bashing in his routines there. However, he did not rule out wisecracks about Iraq's Saddam Hussein.

Leno admitted that it was difficult for any celebrity to entertain the troops and not be looked on as a flag-waver or as too patriotic and cornball for his own good. He said that he felt his role was similar to that of a medic or chaplain— "as long as we don't have Penthouse Pets doing the frug behind me."

Actually, Leno was not the first celebrity to hit the Saudi Arabian sands to inspire the GI's there. Steve Martin and his wife, actress Victoria Tennant, made the trip in October. But Martin was not permitted to put on what would technically be known as a "public entertainment"—since that kind of thing was frowned on by the Arabs on religious grounds.

Martin and his wife confined their activities to mingling with the soldiers and shaking hands and promising to talk to their parents and loved ones back in the States.

The original plans for Leno to entertain at two preselected

spots were soon scrubbed upon closer examination of the complicated logistics involved in just getting him to the combat zone. In the end, Leno and Mavis were flown in by helicopter to twenty different spots around the countryside where he put on ad-libbed shows from the top of tanks and the backs of trucks and the surfaces of flatbeds.

"The desert would get up to a hundred degrees Fahrenheit, a hundred and ten even," Leno said. "I was wearing desert fatigues so I was pretty comfortable, but the hard part to get used to was the great expanse of desert all around."

Leno and Mavis would fly for three hours and see nothing below them but a sea of sand and rolling hills—sand that gleamed like powdered sugar in the hot sunshine.

"When I brushed my teeth," Leno complained, "I spit out sand."

Because of the mandate against "public entertainment," Leno was instructed to get out of the helicopter and confine his activities to walking around among the troops and shaking hands. That kind of simpleminded Robocomic stuff did not sit well with Leno, who liked to use mouth language as well as body language in getting acquainted with people.

"All the guys ever did was walk around all day anyway," Leno pointed out. "They didn't want to see another guy walking around with them!"

And so Leno would climb up on a tank and start to deliver some one-liners. "In a lot of ways, it was like going back to my start in show business, when I'd go into a bar and just stand up and start talking. This is what I envision show business was like in the twelfth century. You just went from caravan to caravan, stood on something, started talking, and hoped a crowd would gather. The one advantage to this was that these guys really had nothing else to do but listen."

When the soldiers would ask him to pose for a picture standing on top of a tank, Leno admitted that he felt a kind of chill run up and down his spine.

"My biggest fear in doing it was that I thought I might look like Michael Dukakis standing on the tank." He did it anyway.

Knowing the typical serviceperson's mind quite well, Leno had prepared some dirty jokes, but when it came to the actual performance, he simply scrubbed them. "The guys didn't seem to want that, which was fine with me."

What he did was the usual: talk about his folks; talk about being on television; talk about Milli Vanilli and lip-synching. And of course, he knew how to wisecrack about the military food and the drawbacks of being in the service.

He'd get out one of the desert lunches and start in on it, look up, and make a surprised face to those nearest him. Then, pointing to the food, he'd say:

"Boy! This stuff is delicious! What is this, Thanksgiving dinner? I can't *believe* you guys are complaining!"

And the troops would start throwing spoons and forks at him.

Actually it was Mavis who got most of the attention. Leno would be struggling to climb out of a tank they had been looking over inside, and a mob of soldiers would be calling out:

"Can I help you, Mrs. Leno?"

Most of the soldiers—male and female—were so young that Mavis herself spoke up later about the fact.

"Twenty years ago," she said, "I'd have been concerned about these guys' girlfriends. Now I'm concerned about their moms."

In town Leno found an entirely different culture—as he had been warned he would. Yet old habits died hard. Whenever Leno traveled, he went out of his way always to be friendly with everyone he met.

"I'd go down the street in Riyadh, the capital of Saudi Arabia, and smile and say 'Hi' to women wearing veils.

They'd look away, and I realized suddenly that this was equivalent to making a pass at them."

"Religion is always tough on a comedian," Leno noted. "I always wince when I watch comedians talking about the Islamic religion, or the way Muslims dress. It's not an area I'm comfortable with. To dismiss an entire culture or religion is really not fair, at least for television."

When he and Mavis went to a restaurant to eat, her presence in public caused the manager to have a screen hauled out and set up around the table. Mavis was told that she should not roll up her shirtsleeves and was instructed to be sure to keep her top button always buttoned.

"If it were blacks they were treating this way instead of women," Leno quoted someone else as saying, "everyone would be up in arms."

Leno decided that the soldiers weren't having all that much fun, either. They were never off gambling or visiting topless bars—since there were neither gambling dens nor topless women within thousands of miles of where they were.

Leno was recognized frequently by Saudi civilians from his appearances on the "Tonight Show," which was shown on local television, weirdly enough, at eleven-thirty in the morning. Leno said that many of them would point at him and say, "Hey, you know Tom Selleck?"

The GI's he visited gave Leno a long list of names to call up when he got back home. When he returned to the States, the comedian made it a point to call up every one of those parents, fiancées, or wives to talk to them about their sons and daughters and loved ones overseas.

"People are so happy that you call, you feel good about it," Leno said.

All in all, the Lenos' trip to the Persian Gulf was considered a major public relations success, and stories about his trip ran everywhere in the press. While that one trip did not make up for Bob Hope's hundreds of similar trips through the years, it did cement the popularity of Jay Leno among young people—something that he had been working on for some time already.

On Saturday, September 14, 1991, Leno was motorcycling along Mulholland Drive in Calabasas when he came upon another cyclist who had stalled on the side of the road. Leno had never yet passed up a cyclist in distress, and he immediately slowed down, signaled for a turn, and started to make a U in the highway to go back to the stalled cycle.

However, at that moment, another motorcycle appeared suddenly, and Leno made a quick turn to swerve out of the way. In the maneuver he went over and in the fall cut and bruised his left leg.

Pretty soon a member of the California Highway Patrol was on hand to straighten out the details, and Leno was taken to Westlake Medical Center where he was treated and then released.

He was said to have been "slightly injured," and it was noted in all the news stories that he had been wearing a helmet—at that time not a requirement of California state law, but certainly a requirement of survival that Leno believed in.

On Tuesday, when he appeared for his stint on the "Tonight Show," Leno hobbled out from the curtains on crutches. As he took his place in the center of the "Tonight" stage, he waited for the applause and the gasps of shock at his crutches to subside before he spoke.

"If I came out and did the monologue on a stool, people would say I've gone Hollywood."

Cheers.

That was the week of September 16. The weekend of September 21 was also a part of the same accident-to-celebrities week. But this time the victim was none other than Leno's old friend and colleague David Letterman!

Letterman did not appear at all on Monday night's "Late Night," but *did* make it to September 24's show on Tuesday. He confessed then that he, too, had been involved in an accident in Florida over the weekend—an automobile accident.

"When your life flashes before you when you're in an accident," he told his audience, "it's a rerun." That was the buildup to the punch line. The punch line? "Technically, I should be *paid* for that."

Letterman then told his audience that he always carried a card in his wallet on which is written: "In case of emergency, notify the stranger living in my house." This was an in joke referring to a woman who frequently broke into his New Canaan, Connecticut, house, fancying herself a fixture in Letterman's private life.

Breaking away from the humorous, Letterman then proceeded to give genuine thanks to the St. Petersburg, Florida, police and fire departments as well as the EMTs and emergency-room workers at Bayfront Hospital in St. Petersburg.

About his injuries and the extent of them, he said that some stitches had been taken.

"You'll have to guess where. But I'll give you a hint. They help my toupee."

Then he beamed a Letterman beam and cracked:

"On the bright side, when you have a rental car and are in an accident, you don't need to return the car." Pause. "It gives new meaning to the term *express check-in.*"

Keep 'em laughing, guys.

Leno hosted the "Tonight Show" all that week in a special arrangement that had been scheduled in advance. By Friday he was standing crutchless. He said then that he would be riding his bike again in about three weeks.

On December 12, 1991, Leno was invited to visit President Bush at the White House. Leno was in town to appear on some shows and promote his third book of comic headlines.

The president said that the visit might provide an opportunity for the comedian to meet the men who gave him much of his comic material—Vice President Quayle, John Sununu, and even George Bush. Sununu had indeed already resigned, but was still cleaning out his desk and had not yet left the White House.

Leno went into the Oval Office armed with a number of jokes of one persuasion or another. When he met the president, the two exchanged greetings and Leno unveiled a particular present he had brought.

It was a joke about Gov. Mario Cuomo, of New York, the man who seemingly could not make up his mind about running for president or not. At the time, Cuomo was saying neither yes nor no to the question that came up constantly at press conferences.

Leno's joke was a terse one-liner:

"Mario Cuomo's public service campaign: 'A mind is a terrible thing to make up.'"

Leno then told the president several jokes about Bush himself. When Bush was asked later what they were, the president said simply, "He had a couple about me, but I can't tell you what they were."

Later Leno was invited to sit in on Marlin Fitzwater's daily briefing of the president. At the end of the briefing, Leno pretended to be one of the reporters sitting in on the briefing by raising his hand and asking:

"Is there any connection between Sununu resigning and Pan Am going under?" Pause. "I mean, they both happened about the same time."

After the laughter, Fitzwater responded, "I've got an answer for that one, but in my business, Jay, sometimes the best jokes you can't say."

Fitzwater then proved he was willing to laugh at himself as much as any other public figure. He responded to Leno's jest with the following mock announcement:

"The president is pleased to announce today that Jay Leno has agreed to run against Pat Buchanan in all the primaries."

Leno raised his eyebrows. "Isn't that the guy from 'Petticoat Junction'? Pat Buchanan? Oh, no, that's Edgar Buchanan. I'm sorry."

In the spirit of fun, Leno was asked, "Do you have any campaign promises to make?"

"We're working on that still," Leno said with that serious vacant face that politicians assume when trying to pontificate without seeming to be pontifical. "That's all being formulated."

"Are you considering an 'America last' approach in rebuttal to President Bush's 'America first' approach?"

Leno thought that one over. "That's pretty much taking care of itself. I think that's all falling into plan."

Later on Leno met Vice President Dan Quayle for the first time. Quayle had been the butt of Leno's humor ever since becoming vice president. Yet Leno told him one about Sen. Ted Kennedy.

Kennedy had just figured in the news recently when his nephew, William Kennedy Smith, was tried and acquitted of a rape charge in West Palm Beach.

"What did Teddy say when he heard the verdict?" Leno asked. Then he went into his wide-beaming grin: "'PAR-TEE! PAR-TEE!'"

The vice president and Leno exchanged some repartee in which Quayle suggested he get some of the residuals from Leno for all the jokes made up at his expense. Later Quayle said that he had requested that Leno "ease up" a bit on the Quayle quips.

Nevertheless, when Leno left, Quayle told him, "If you ever get in trouble for material, let me know and I'll try to help you out."

Late in January 1992, Jay Leno was working in Chicago

when he happened to drive by the site of a new hotel, where he spotted a long line of three thousand people waiting in the snow and freezing temperatures to apply for a thousand jobs at the newly built hostelry.

"He was depressed about it," said Rick Uchwat, a friend of Leno's, and the owner of four comedy clubs in the city.

Leno and Uchwat worked out a deal. Leno would do two separate shows at one of Uchwat's comedy clubs for the unemployed. No admission would be necessary. Only proof of unemployment compensation would be required for two tickets. Soft drinks would be served free, with the proceeds from alcohol sales to go to a homeless shelter in Chicago. The shows were presented February 13 and 14. Again, the public relations ploy registered in the high 10s.

Ironically enough, on the day after Jay Leno's motorcycle mishap, a publicity story about him appeared in the *Boston Globe*. Written by Nathan Cobb, it contained a revealing anecdote, with the startling kind of coincidental tie-in that happens only in real life.

It seemed that Leno and Cobb were driving back to Boston after a show Leno had appeared in. They were in the Lincoln Continental that Leno had bought for his father. Leno was at the wheel. He was working his way up Route 3 toward home and was hitting a speed a little over the fifty-five-mile-an-hour speed limit.

A Massachusetts state trooper came out of the blue to flag him over to the side of the highway. Cobb watched with interest as the confrontation proceeded.

The trooper stuck his flashlight into Leno's eyes, asking him the usual questions. Leno then reached for his wallet and began taking out everything he could think of to impress the trooper and plead his cause.

Item: honorary police membership cards.

The trooper was unconvinced, if not downright unimpressed.

Item: a United States Treasury Department badge.

The trooper shrugged that one off without comment.

Item: a card Leno carried in case he was captured by the enemy in Saudi Arabia.

The trooper was interested, but not really all *that* interested.

Cobb, the journalist, wrote: "He's not being Jay Leno, star. He's being Jamie Leno, a teenager caught speeding in his father's car and hoping no one will find out."

Now the trooper took the material in his hands and began looking it over with some amusement. "Well, you're covering all the bases here," he commented.

Leno was all wide-eyed and innocent. A lamb at the slaughter. The last plea. "Yeah, yeah. Oh, I'm sorry about this, sir. Real sorry."

The trooper was examining the treasury medal. "What *is* this?"

"President Bush gave me that for going to Saudi Arabia, sir."

The trooper nodded, bemused. "You've got everything here."

"Yeah. I'm sorry, sir."

The trooper looked at Leno. "How fast were you going back there?"

Leno would rather not have been asked to guess. For once he had nothing to say.

The trooper cleared his throat.

"I don't know," Leno said quickly. He made an effort to concentrate. At least, that was the story his face told. "I was probably going about"—a long, long pause—"about sixty-two, maybe. I guess. Miles an hour."

"Sixty-two?" the trooper repeated. Then, like an auctioneer: "How about seventy-two?"

Leno's eyes widened. "Was I going—*that* fast?" Pause. "I'm sorry, sir."

The trooper sifted through the findings once more, shrugging. "Jeez, I gotta give you something." He looked at Leno. "My wife will never believe me."

Leno did what he found it hard to do. He said nothing. He simply looked at the trooper. Pleading his cause.

The trooper took out his pad and began writing in it. Leno's face fell. He tried to smile, but his face—usually so pliable and obedient—wouldn't work. The trooper handed over the pad for Leno to sign. Leno read it by the light of the dashboard. The citation was a warning, stating that Leno had been traveling an illegal sixty-four miles an hour—not the seventy-two miles an hour the trooper had originally cited, but not the sixty-two Leno had either.

The trooper went over the cards and medals and Leno slowly put them back in his wallet. The trooper then slapped his pad shut and gave both Leno and Cobb a cheery good-night. He vanished and they could hear him climb on his bike, gun it up, and disappear to the rear of the Lincoln.

When the trooper was out of sight and hearing, Leno started up his father's car, and during the rest of the trip back to Andover, never did more than fifty-five miles an hour.

Cobb ended his story:

"As he pulls onto the highway, however, he looks across the seat and cracks a sly little smile, looking every bit the kid who just avoided being hauled off to the principal's office."

And then Leno made a remark that seemed to Cobb to sum up the story of Leno's life: "Show business is great."

14

Leno on Comedy

A HUMORIST IS, above all, a philosopher of life who has that special ability to make people laugh, a commentator who can expose the foibles and follies of life, impart a sense of the ludicrous to the idiocies surrounding us all, and inspire in us the urge to laugh at them rather than fear them.

Leno is a philosopher with a sense of humor, a philosopher whose fables and adages will live on long after he is gone for the enjoyment of future generations.

In these latter decades of the fast-fading twentieth century, Jay Leno has proved himself to be a master satirist, a superb craftsman of the comic thrust, a prototype of the modern-day philosopher-satirist.

His apperceptions, his concerns, and his comments—most of them wry—on the crazy world we live in today come forth vividly in conversations he carries on, about humor, about what comedy is, and about the importance of comedians in helping the world retain its sanity. There is nothing Jay Leno likes to talk about more than comedy—and the art of making people laugh. His observations are endless. Here are a few of them.

To Leno, being on the stage doing comedy is the most relaxing and refreshing thing he could possibly do. "It's the most soothing, calming part of the day. I mean, you're onstage, you have no problems, nothing. You're seeing smiling faces, people at their best. Most people don't see three thousand people in a day, let alone three thousand people who are smiling and laughing all the time. I'm always more rested after a show than before it."

Unlike some celebrities in the business of comedy, Leno *likes* being recognized by his fans. "The difference, I guess, is that they recognize me as *me*, not as some character I play on TV or in the movies. I guess that's why people aren't disappointed when they meet me. I'm the same person on TV or in person. It's fun. But what's so unbelievable is that they are actually paying me money to have this much fun. I can't believe it."

A lot of comedy, according to Leno, comes from anger, from people who have had a bad childhood and have a *desire* to get back at the world. "I like the world," Leno says. "I've always been very content with it. I never understood the anger of Lenny Bruce. He was never the hero to me that he was to many of my friends." Leno's friends would say, "Oh, man, he went and told that audience off and walked off the stage!" Leno's attitude was different. "Why didn't he stay on the stage and get them to laugh?"

Leno: "I just never got it. I mean, you can go into this with two agendas, really. Some people go in with the agenda of 'I have a message, and if they don't get it, screw 'em.' Or you can say, 'I'm there to make people laugh, so let's see what I can do.'

"I'm not out there to espouse my personal views. I'm out there to make people laugh. I don't think anyone could figure out my political bent by watching my show. Which is a plus, if you're going to do a national show."

As for whether he's a Republican or a Democrat, Leno has a standard answer. "I'm neither, actually. I try to remain a staunch independent, because every time I think I'm a

Republican, they do something greedy, and every time I think I'm a Democrat, they do something stupid."

Leno grew up lucky with loving parents and lots of friends—requisites for a decent, healthy outlook on life." I don't say comedians have to work clean to be funny. Not at all. They can work any way they want. I work clean because it seems to be the revolutionary thing to do now."

Consistency is a must for good comedy, Leno believes. "A lot of times when I used to go to the Catskills, I'd watch neophyte comedians—guys in their early twenties. In the beginning of their act, their wife is fat and ugly and awful to sleep with, and then, eight jokes later, they've got a gag about how their wife's a nympho. 'Make up your mind!' I'm thinking. 'Where are you coming from?' Early on, I decided to make sure that my stuff sticks to what I am or what my point of view is."

It turns out that everybody in the world wants to do comedy—and thinks he or she is a talented comedian just naturally. "I'm always running into people—including one U.S. Senator—who tell me they're dying to perform stand-up. I listen to them and they sound funny enough. But when they finally get up the nerve to go on stage on an amateur night at some comedy club, they stop being themselves and are afraid to go with the kind of stuff they were telling me. They switch to generic scatological humor and basic jokes and fall flat on their faces. They aren't funny anymore and they can't understand why not."

It takes a mainstream comedian to fill up the theaters where Leno performs. "If I were not a mainstream comedian, most places would be only about half-full. You have a lot of people out there over the age of fifty, and you have a lot of people under the age of thirty. In this economy, you're not going to attract all of the people in either one of those groups. So you need *everybody*."

What comedy is all about is a simple matter. "You get out

there and tell jokes," Leno says. "If they laugh, you get paid. If they don't laugh, you don't get paid. It's about as basic a business as you can get. With the exception of the microphone, the level of technology is zero. It hasn't changed, really, since the Council of Trent. One guy gets up and talks, the other people listen. It's as ancient, low-tech, and primitive as there is. Except for the occasional snaillike pace of the language, there's really no progress."

As for a new breed of comedians surfacing today, Leno shrugs his shoulders. "I don't see anybody breaking new ground in comedy. There was a joke book written about 1710, literally. It's English and you see versions of all those jokes you've heard all your life, about the guy on his wedding night . . . every one of them.

"You realize that comedy is not all that different now. There are only so many variations of it. If I asked you to sit down and watch a silent movie from the twenties—a love story or action adventure—I don't think you could watch it for more than ten minutes. But if I put on a Chaplin, Keaton, or Keystone Kops, you'd probably laugh as much as the people laughed then.

"That's the nature of comedy. It's not like music. There isn't new technology coming into it or new sounds. Cheech and Chong and their drug jokes are really Ted Lewis and his alcohol jokes. Comedy is all the fat lady at the opera or the rich, pompous guy getting his comeuppance when he slips on a banana peel.

"People say—'Oh, you're doing something different.' I'm not doing anything *different*. I'm just trying to do it well."

Leno is philosophical about the amount of traveling he has to do in the business of entertaining people. "I don't like traveling," he says, "but that's how you find out if your jokes are really funny."

In addition, he points out, "Hip—'in'—humor is what

happens within fifty miles of your home. I travel so much my humor's generic."

But there is one area he stays away from when he travels. "I never fly first class because nothing funny ever happens in first class."

In Leno's eyes, ticking off an audience is *not* what comedy is all about. "I was once asked why I was afraid to tick off my audience." Leno shakes his head. "They're my audience! Why would I *want* to tick them off?" Leno throws up his hands in defeat. "I just don't understand the logic there. To me, if you're a comedian, you should make everybody laugh. Everybody. Case closed."

In his career, Leno has been in every city in the United States, as he says, at least once. "I don't mean *kind of* every city. I mean *every city*. This business is a bit like being an athlete. You have fifteen or twenty years where you put out and people want to see you. And you can't keep coming back year after year, even with new material, because people finally say, 'Well, we already saw you.'"

Leno was once asked why he never slowed down to enjoy life. His response was that he did not consider working at all offensive. "When you work for yourself, you have the advantage of saying what you want to say." To Leno, self-expression is a form of enjoyment in itself.

One night Leno was about to make fun of a guy in the audience who was wearing a silly hat. When Leno asked the man who he was, the man said, "I run this place." Leno responded instantly, "Well, that's an excellent hat, sir. And a fine, fine head."

Comedy, Leno says, is a business to which the performer has to adapt. "I opened for Perry Como on a summer tour once. There was no way I was going to get away with a lot of blue material. I was glad that I could work to that audience. A comedian should be able to make *everybody* laugh."

Leno never had any plans to make a comedy album for people to listen to. "Comedy's not like music," he says. "Listening to a comedy album is like watching a dog eat. You just take as much as you can, and then you drop dead. You're sick of it. When I bought a comedy album in college, I would play it fifty times a day for my friends. We'd all laugh at the same phrase or the same joke. And then I'd just smash it. I couldn't *stand to listen to it anymore.* "Comedy is a shared experience. You have to be in a room with other people who feel the same way you do. My attitude has always been, if you want to hear it, I'll come to your town and do it for you."

Leno once reminisced about what it was like to appear in a strip joint when he was starting out in his career. "A lot of businessmen on their one night out a year were in the crowd. They were a fairly bright audience. I could get off some clever lines, and there were lots of nude girls running around. I'll have to admit, I didn't find it particularly depressing."

About the comedians who make him laugh the most, Leno once said: "Robert Klein, Johnny Carson, David Letterman—some of the younger comedians like Jerry Seinfeld, Steve Wright, Carol Leifer, Elayne Boosler—I like people who use words effectively. I don't like the 'pie-in-the-face' comedians. Guys who put on a dress. That kind of thing."

Leno once tried to analyze what motivates him in being a comedian. "I honestly don't know. My grandfather was an Italian immigrant. I always felt that restlessness to be somewhere else. Back east I'm that crazy comedian from California, but here [in California] I'm the straightest guy in the world. I don't smoke or drink or do drugs. Maybe it's an inferiority thing with my older brother, who went to Yale and was one of the ten smartest students in the country.

"I have an adventurous spirit. It's one of the things that makes the West Coast different from the East Coast. My dad was in his fifties before we could really talk. He was a child of the Depression. I guess I've inherited the fear of being broke. . . .

Leno has said again and again that he *likes* people. And, of course, he wants people to like him. Since much comic humor involves putting people down, it is difficult to avoid offending all the time. Yet other great comics, Leno points out, have succeeded. "People *love* Red Skelton, Bob Hope. For people to just like you, that's ninety-nine percent of the struggle."

The toughest thing about being recognized as a comedian is to *stay* funny. "After you've made a name for yourself, people expect more," Leno says. "And sometimes, when there's nothing funny in the papers, I guess I do get a little edgy about the future. But that doesn't happen very often."

"Ask Jay Leno where he gets his material, and he'll tell you," wrote Mark Faris in the *Akron Beacon Journal.* "He'll tell you he steals it. Says he just goes to a small town, finds a club that has a comic, and takes down the gags line for line."

But then, what comic is anything but a big kidder?

In fact, as Faris added in his newspaper piece, "Leno . . . is, of course, just kidding—at least he *says* he is."

Leno once discussed the particular subjects that a comedian can use to make people laugh. "I have a good family, a good background, a good marriage. So those are the things that most of my humor represents. Now, if a comedian comes from a broken home, had alcoholic parents, or something like that, his or her humor will reflect that. And that's okay with me—as long as it isn't contrived."

Is comedy easier to do today than it was yesterday? Or is it harder? "In some ways," Leno says, "it's harder to do comedy these days because the public's attention span is very, very short. When you look at stand-up comedians from the sixties or the fifties, you had a lot of storytellers who would come out and, in a five-minute chunk, maybe only hit two or three laughs, but it was this whole woven, amusing story. But Rodney Dangerfield, he's the perfect TV comic. He comes out, bang-bang-bang-bang-bang, and he's gone.

"People nod off real quick. I mean, look at newspaper stories. Everything is just three or four paragraphs . . . the basic facts. There is so much news that people actually know *less*. Years ago, if something happened, you'd stay on that issue for weeks and weeks and weeks, and you'd learn a lot about that issue.

"Today, you just get inundated with information."

It is possible to perform too much? "The idea," Leno says, "is not to fall into the Peter Principle—in the sense that, if you're used to working every night, you're sharper than if you play once a week. A lot of comics figure, well, I'll just do one night instead of working the week. Then they think they're doing so well they cut back to working just twice a month. Then once every two months. Pretty soon, you don't have any act left.

"I think I work just as much. I just jump around to different markets. Instead of working seven nights in Indianapolis, I'll work seven cities in and around that area."

Asked if he was still a comedian in his off hours—those few he has—Leno remarked, "I don't crawl into bed wearing a plaid jacket or anything like that. I try to keep in a reasonable frame of mind at home. Actually, my life is pretty normal, pretty much like everybody else's, I suppose."

He does believe that a comedian in public should always be a comedian. "I know when I was a kid and was watching for my favorite comedian on a show, and he'd just come on and sit there and talk and not be funny, I'd be disappointed. And so I always want to be funny. I don't want to go on a game show or judge something."

He likes the fact that his humor tends to have a strong blue-collar appeal. "Not from the point of being dirty," he says, "but from the point of being stuff that everybody can understand."

Hatred has no place in comedy. "Whether it's directed at blacks or Jews or gays, or whatever, I don't like seeing people united in hatred. Better be united in love or laughter. I don't mean to sound hokey, but I don't want to come out of a comedy show thinking the world is an awful place and we should all just die. I like to come out feeling good about things."

It's not individuals he prefers to satirize, but institutions or groups of individuals. "I think it's more fun to go after the *system* than after the individual. It's a cheap shot to make fun of blacks or gays, but fun to make fun of a system that allows the kinds of things that happen to these people to happen."

His fans frequently bring him jokes to use. "Here's a cute story," someone will say, and then he'll tell probably the filthiest, raunchiest story you can imagine. "Or he'll tell you another comedian's joke, and say it's okay for you to use it. *Sure* it is." Pause. "Not."

Leno gets recognized a lot more than he was before he made the "Tonight Show." "It's great fun, actually. I *like* people, so I don't mind this. It's not like I'm a rock star so that people maul me."

Doing comedy sitcoms is not Leno's idea of fun time. After a scene was shot he once complained that he was not happy with the joke. But the members of the crew waved him off.

"Don't worry. We'll fix it in postproduction," they told him.

Leno frowned. "But it's not funny."

The crewmen said, "Just wait until you see it on the air. It'll get a big laugh."

To Leno, it was a strange way to get any laugh—big or little.

Leno has never really settled down or understood

the West Coast life. It's not only the laid-back attitude every-one has, but the transient quality of everything that baffles him.

"My wife's from here," he says, "and not only is her high school gone, but the hill her high school was on is gone! But there are advantages to L.A. You can get *People* magazine here on Sunday. In Andover, they don't get it until Thursday."

Leno believes that the comic muse is strong in Boston, where he spent most of his growing-up years—stronger than on the West Coast, for example. Or at least, it's different.

"You see it in comics like Steven Wright, Lenny Clarke, and some others," Leno says. "It's that Yankee sarcasm that you don't get in other parts of the country. Guys from New England have a certain kind of distrust. I know for myself, whenever I hear a statement from a politician, I always try to figure out what it *really* means. That comes from growing up in New England."

But there are other cities with good comedy traditions. Leno does not follow W. C. Fields in his negative assessment of Philadelphia. Fields loathed playing Philly. Leno loves it—"It's a great town," he told *Philadelphia* magazine in 1985. He went on:

"My favorite [comedy] cities are Philly, Boston, and San Francisco. I find the audiences to be very hip, very cosmo-politan. You can make fun of the people and the city and they seem to like that. They don't take themselves as seriously as they do in New York. You can't insult New Yorkers; they get very upset."

It's the unintentional humor in some films that moves Leno to laughter—faster than the intentional kind. "You're watching a gangster movie, and the guy is on the run, and he checks into a cheap hotel. He *always* gets a room up front, next to that flashing red VACANCY sign. If I were on the run, I'd want a room at the *back,* as far back as I could get!"

Leno once had this to say about the difference between the "Tonight Show" and the "Letterman" show: "'Letterman' is a comedy show that happens to have guests. The 'Tonight Show' is a talk show that happens to have comedy."

Leno has his own theory about the impact of comedy on politics. "I don't think it has an impact." A joke, he says, is a joke. "I mean, if the joke is funny, people laugh. Thank you. Good-bye. I mean, it's a joke. I'm a comedian. I'm not really a political satirist."

As for comedy, generally: "I like to write jokes, tell them, and go home. Comedy is like golf: if you can play it right, you can do it for a long time."

Epilogue

T HE MEDIA BLITZ unleashed by NBC in anticipation of Jay Leno's opening night as star of the "Tonight Show" on May 25, 1992, was truly awesome. No expense was spared. Stories began appearing in the print medium as early as February 1992. Electronic appearances began in March and continued up to and including opening night.

How could anyone escape the fact that Jay Leno was, in *Time* magazine's alliterative style, "Midnight Mayor."

Indeed the promo stories individually—especially the quaint angles conceived to puff Jay Leno—proved marvelously ingenious.

Item: In January, *Broadcasting* ran a short take on Edd Hall, Leno's new voice-over announcer. Of course, Jay Leno was the actual anchor of the piece.

Item: In February, *People* magazine picked up a bit from a book by Nancy Cobb titled *How They Met,* featuring Mavis Leno rather than Jay, but subliminally centering on him. To take the edge off the promotional ploy, *People* ran a number of other pieces from the same book, which told stories of married celebrities and their first moments together.

Item: In March, Jay Leno appeared on the cover of *Time* magazine with an accompanying story that was very flattering to him and that ran side by side with a farewell-to-Johnny story about Carson's thirty years as the late-night king of TV.

Item: In April, Arsenio Hall, annoyed at the enormous amount of publicity garnered by the Leno camp, published an interview in *Entertainment Weekly* in which he took his soon-to-be competitor to task for several magazine stories calling the two of them longtime friends. Hall apparently felt that Leno was patronizing him. "Jay and I are *not* friends," he pointed out. He warned Leno that when the two squared off as competitors in the late-night talk-show sweepstakes, he was going to "kick Jay's ass. So get ready for me!" Feuds between entertainers are always good for publicity and viewer interest. In succeeding stories and interviews, Leno spent a good deal of time reminiscing about his relationship with Hall, mentioning the time he had invited Hall and his mother to his house. However, if Hall wanted it known that they were not friends, that was all right with Leno.

Item: In April, *TV Guide* ran a big story on Leno, titled "Jay Leno: Is He Up to It?" In it Digby Diehl chided the comedian for deliberately dulling the cutting edge of his comedy in order to be everybody's court jester. If anything, the attack fueled interest in how Leno would handle his material in his new role as late-night star.

Item: In early May, the *New York Post* did what might be considered a David Letterman treatment of the "Tonight Show" by writing a takeout on the company in New York that had produced the filmed "opening" for the Jay Leno show—with the camera swishing through curtain after curtain as if Leno were making his way through hundreds of stages to appear finally in front of the audience.

And of course there was much more than that.

Even so, the print impress paled during the last days before May 25, when some of the biggest shows on television suddenly took notice of Jay Leno.

In March 1992, Leno was interviewed on "60 Minutes" by Steve Kroft. This turned out to be a fairly general conversation about Leno's comedic outlook, compared to Carson's. The show is the top-rated magazine of the air. Now in May, the television medium blitz stepped up its pace. On May 11, Jay Leno apepared on "Oprah," interviewed by Oprah Winfrey for the full hour. One of the most memorable moments occurred in a taped accolade for Leno by Rosie O'Donnell, a comedian. She recalled how she had opened for the first time as an emcee at the Governor's Comedy Club, Long Island, when she was just nineteen. Leno was headlining. "I get up, I do my five minutes," Rosie said. "I'm not very funny. He goes up, does his show, two hours. He's *very* funny." Afterward he walked over to her and smiled. "What is this, your first time? You're doing real good out there. You know—if you change that joke around there, I think it would work a little better, but keep up the good work! You're really doing good!" O'Donnell concluded: "He was really nice to me. And the moral of the story is, sometimes nice guys finish first."

On May 12, Leno appeared on the "Barbara Walters Show" on ABC-TV. He shared the spotlight with Johnny Carson. Walters said of them: "Johnny and Jay are Hollywood institutions with mainstream tastes." That set the theme for the segment.

Nine days later, Jay Leno was interviewed on the "Later with Bob Costas" show, which airs at 1:30 A.M. following the "David Letterman Show." For two full hours, Costas and Leno chatted together about various phases of Leno's life and career. Leno plugged his show, particularly in the selection of Branford Marsalis as musical director. He also illustrated his footwork in the comedic vein. Costas asked him: "What do you think's the key to staying power and what's the definition of staying power?" Leno, quick as a wink: "Oysters." Leno also pointed out that in 1962 the critics were as rough on Carson as they were in 1992 on Leno. Their complaint then as well as now: "Oh, he's [Carson was then; Leno is now] too easy on the guests."

On May 25, Leno appeared on the "Today Show," interviewed by Katie Couric. It was the morning of his initial appearance that night as permanent star of the "Tonight Show." Leno got another chance to plug Marsalis and the show in general. He also took Arsenio Hall to task for his part in the so-called feud between them. He spun a yarn about his appearance on Oprah Winfrey's show. After he was through, he said, he went back to the green room to get his stuff. Four men surrounded him, saying they were great fans, and asked for autographs. On the way to the parking lot with someone, Leno asked a member of the show who those "great fans of his" were. "They're on the next Oprah show," his informant said. "They're men who have murdered their wives."

The next morning, Leno was interviewed on "Today" again, this time by Stone Phillips. After some inside material about the show the night before, Leno had this to say about "opening night": "It's a bit like buying a house and then kind of remodeling and stuff."

How did the public and the critics take the "remodeling and stuff"?

The *New York Post* did a rundown of Leno's stand-up routine:

The obligatory Dan Quayle joke: The "Tonight Show" is the show that the vice president "hates even more than 'Murphy Brown.'"

The obligatory Murphy Brown joke: "One thing you can say about Murphy Brown that you can't say about Dan Quayle: She'll be back in the fall."

The obligatory Ross Perot joke: "The less he says the more popular he gets." Pause. "Which is something that Dan Quayle has yet to grasp."

The obligatory joke inserted at the beginning of the stand-up after being greeted enthusiastically by the crowd: "Let's see how you all feel in thirty years."

New York Times TV critic John J. O'Connor commented on the mixture of comedian Billy Crystal and Robert Krulwich, a satirical TV observer of the economics scene. Although it was obvious that Leno was trying to prove that he could mix the serious with the comic, O'Connor wrote: "It's possible, but a lot more work is required on context and transitions. Monday's awkward juxtaposition was unfair to Mr. Crystal, Mr. Krulwich, and the loyal but no doubt puzzled viewers."

Jeff Jarvis wrote a highly critical review in *TV Guide*, pointing out that Leno seemed to be doing everything he could to be liked by everyone. Leno even had the audacity to give himself a good review at the end of his initial stint: "Not bad, if I do say so myself." Later in the week, Leno warned his viewers that the "Tonight Show" was not the same show their parents had watched.

Jarvis: "Fine, Jay, you're not Johnny. But who are you? That's the problem."

He criticized Leno for trying to milk laughs with a kind of "practiced sheepishness and aren't-I-cute grins," assessed his monologue as "second-rate" and his interviews as "lifeless catalogues of biographical anecdotes, not conversations."

Noting that Leno would soon be contending with heavyweights in the late-night arena—naming Arsenio Hall, David Letterman, Dennis Miller, and soon Chevy Chase and Whoopi Goldberg—Jarvis concluded: "I can't help feeling sorry for him. He's not bad. He's just sad."

Jet magazine's Clarence Waldron in June 1992 praised the show's music. "Marsalis has composed a new theme song, which he describes as more funky than jazzy." But, he said, there was more to the show than brilliant music.

"The show is a hit because of the warm rapport between Leno and Marsalis. With Leno's clean, inoffensive brand of humor and Marsalis's cool, charming, winning personality, the show is already winning rave reviews from TV critics and is keeping millions glued to their TV sets every night. TV fans just like these two guys."

Marsalis, *Jet* said, did not consider "The Arsenio Hall Show" competition. "It's really like apples and oranges. It's just a different show."

Waldron: "Leno and Marsalis are indeed continuing the 'Tonight Show's' legacy of good taste and quality entertainment in a big way. Late-night TV just doesn't get any better than this."

The Nielsen ratings after the show opened tended to prove critic Waldron right. The initial Leno show had a rating of 13.9 in the nation's twenty-five largest cities, each point representing 921,000 homes. He reached 38 percent of all viewers watching television at that time. By comparison, Carson was averaging a 5.2 percent rating and a 16 percent share of late-night viewers during his last year.

That rating was earned in spite of the fact that in the Eastern and Central time zones the show went on after midnight because of the National Basketball Assocation's playoff schedule.

Jay Leno is a survivor, as he has proved from the start of his career. The odds are that he will continue to be so.

Bibliography

Amstead, Alicia. "Jay Leno: The Face That's Launched a Thousand Quips." *Bangor Daily News*, July 19, 1990.

Anderson, Dale. "Joke All You Want, He'll Make More." *Buffalo News*, Aug. 20, 1989.

Armstrong, David. "American-Made Comedy: Jay Leno Has a Laugh on the Country." *San Francisco Examiner*, July 4, 1988.

Azizian, Carol A. "Jay Leno." *Flint* (Mich.) *Journal*, July 21, 1991.

Barol, Bill. "An American Comedy." *Newsweek*, June 2, 1986.

Barr, Robert. "'Tonight' Is Tops with Leno." *New York Daily News*, July 20, 1987.

Beck, Marilyn. "Leno Says 'Tonight' Will Get Political." *TV Guide*, Dec. 28, 1991.

Bickelhaupt, Susan. "A New Day for 'Tonight'; Leno to Succeed Carson, May Lure Younger Audience." *Boston Globe*, June 7, 1991.

———. "Leno Gets Laughs on His Home Turf." *Boston Globe*, Aug. 5, 1991.

Billard, Mary. "Jawing with Jay Leno." *Gentlemen's Quarterly*, Aug. 1989.

Blakey, Bob. "Leno Had Tears of Mirth Flowing." *Calgary Herald*, Nov. 21, 1991.

Borns, Betsy. "Jay Leno Takes It on the Chin." *Mademoiselle*, Oct. 1988.

Boss, Kit. "Dennis Miller: Perfect Postmodern Talk-Show Host." *Seattle Times*, Feb. 29, 1992.

Brennan, Patricia. "Live! From L.A.! It's Jay Leno's New Year's Eve!" *Washington Post*, Dec. 30, 1990.

Brooks, Tim, and Earle Marsh. *The Complete Directory to Prime Time Network TV Shows*. New York: Ballantine Books, 1979–1988.

Brown, Joe. "Jay Leno." *Washington Post*, June 25, 1982.

Buck, Jerry. "Jay Leno Looks for Canine-Nipping Homo Sapiens." *Associated Press*, Sept. 23, 1985.

209

Bussard, Camron E. "Jokes? He's Got a Million of 'Em. Motorcycles? He's Working on It." *Cycle World*, May 1989.

Carman, John. "'Tonight' Show Is All Leno's." *San Francisco Chronicle*, June 7, 1991.

Carter, Bill. "High Rating for Len's First Night." *New York Times*, May 27, 1992.

————. "NBC Appoints Jay Leno to Replace Johnny Carson." *New York Times*, June 7, 1991.

Carter, Graydon. "Jay Leno, the King of Stand-up Comedy. . . ." *Rolling Stone*, Nov. 2, 1989.

Christon, Lawrence. "Realist Comic Jay Leno Is Thinking All the Time." *Los Angeles Times*, June 16, 1986.

————. "Jay Leno—Spokesman for the Exploited American Everyman." *Los Angeles Times*, Feb. 4, 1988.

————. "On the Road with America's Hardest-Working Comedian." *Los Angeles Times*, Oct. 22, 1989.

Cobb, Nancy. *How They Met.* New York: Turtle Bay Books, 1992.

Cobb, Nathan. "Nice Guys Finish First." *Boston Globe*, Sept. 15, 1991.

"Comic Jay Leno Gets His Laughs All by Himself." *Chicago Tribune*, Dec. 28, 1987.

Cooper, Ann. "The Class of Clowns: Nobody's Hotter Than Comic Jay Leno." *Advertising Age*, July 21, 1986.

Corcoran, Patti. "Jay Leno." *People*, Nov. 30, 1987.

Corliss, Richard. "Passing the Late-Night Crown." *Time*, June 17, 1991.

Coto, Juan Carlos. "Leno: Comedy Is an 'Easy' Job." *Miami Herald*, Nov. 25, 1988.

Cunningham, Kim. "Fast Times at Andover High." *People*, Mar. 23, 1992.

"Declaration of War." *Los Angeles Times*, Apr. 10, 1992.

Devault, Russ. "Jay Leno's 'Collision Course.'" *Atlanta Journal*, Apr. 4, 1987.

De Vries, Hilary. "Rubber-Faced Jay Leno Pulls Laughs out of Life." *Christian Science Monitor*, Dec. 22, 1986.

Diehl, Digby. "Jay Leno: Is He up to It?" *TV Guide*, Apr. 11, 1992.

Doggrell, Glenn. "Comedy Review: Laughs Never Stop with Leno." *Los Angeles Times*, June 1, 1991.

Driscoll, Kathi Scrizzi. "Super Sub." *Cape Cod Times* (Hyannis, Mass.), July 15, 1989.

Du Brow, Rick. "Leno: Keeper of the Flame in Hot Seat." *Los Angeles Times*, June 15, 1991.

Endrst, James. "Jay Leno Has First Special in Prime Time." *Hartford Courant*, Nov. 21, 1987.

Ervolino, Bill. "A Word with Jay Leno." *New York Post*, Aug. 3, 1988.

Faris, Mark. "Leno Isn't Big-Headed over Big-Time Status." *Akron Beacon Journal*, Sept. 28, 1989.

Forrest, Susan. "Andover to 'Tonight Show.'" *Lawrence* (Mass.) *Eagle-Tribune*. Oct. 23, 1988.

Galloway, Stephen, Mary Murphy, and Timothy Carlson. "Look Who's Scrambling to Become the Next King of Late-Night TV." *TV Guide*, June 29, 1991.

Goldstein, Marianne. "Johnny Who? Heeeeeeeere's Jay," *New York Post*, May 26, 1992.

Graham, Jefferson. "Leno's Funny Business: Comedian Scans 'Headlines' for Humor." *USA Today*, Dec. 5, 1989.

———. "Through Thick and Thin Leno and Agent Kushnick Forge Strong Ties Sharing the Stardom and the Sorrows." *USA Today*, Dec. 10, 1991.

———. "Jay Leno Gets Ready to Put His Own Stamp on the Show." *USA Today*, Apr. 14, 1992.

Green, Tom. "Late Night with Jay Leno." *Cosmopolitan*, Oct. 1986.

Greppi, Michele. "Jay Leno to Visit Letterman Show." *New York Daily News*, Dec. 13, 1991.

Harpo Productions, Inc. "Oprah." *Transcript*, May 11, 1992.

Hastings, Deborah. "'It Beats Having a Day Job,' Jay Leno Says of Hosting 'Tonight Show.'" *Associated Press*, June 7, 1991.

"Heeeeeeere's Jay!" *Stamford* (Conn.) *Advocate*. Jan. 29, 1992.

Hill, Michael E. "Jay Leno Giving NBC Prime Time a Try with His 'Family Comedy Hour' Special." *Newark Star-Ledger*, Nov. 23, 1987.

Hodenfield, Chris. "Motor Mouth." *Cycle*, Feb. 1987.

"Honesty Is Always the Best Policy, Part Two." *Los Angeles Times*, Apr. 12, 1992.

Hughes, Mike. "Carson Quitting in Ninety-two; Leno Likely Successor?" *Gannett News Service*, May 24, 1991.

Isaacs, Barbara. "Jay Leno: The Nice Guy of Stand-up Comedy." *Rochester* (N.Y.) *Democrat and Chronicle*, Nov. 5, 1989.

Jarvis, Jeff. "Jay Leno's 'Tonight Show.'" *TV Guide*, June 27, 1992.

"Jay Leno." *Current Biography Yearbook*, 1988.

"Jay Leno." *New York Daily News*, June 14, 1987.

"Jay Leno Headlining at Caesars Palace through Tonight." *Los Angeles Times*, Sept. 1, 1991.

"Jay Leno: He's Serious about Humor." *Denver Post*, May 14, 1989.

"Jay Leno Injured in Motorcycle Accident." *Los Angeles Times*, Sept. 16, 1991.

"Jay Leno Injured in Motorcycle Accident." *Washington Times*, Sept. 16, 1991.

"Jay Leno: King of the Three-Liners." *Philadelphia* magazine, Nov. 1985.

"Jay Leno Makes Calls for GIs." *Los Angeles Times*, Dec. 17, 1990.

"Jay Leno Slightly Injured in Crash." *Montreal Gazette*, Sept. 16, 1991.

"Jay Leno's New Edd-ition." *People*, Mar. 23, 1992.

"Jay Leno to Entertain Troops in Persian Gulf." *United Press International*, Sept. 6, 1990.

"Jobless Benefit." *USA Today*, Jan. 23, 1992.

Johnson, Dean. "Leno Laughs Off Stardom." *Boston Herald,* Aug. 30, 1990.

Johnson, Peter. "Letterman Laughs Off Anger about 'Tonight.'" *USA Today,* Sept. 3, 1991.

———. "Leno Will Hang On to His Crutches for Another Week." *USA Today,* Sept. 23, 1991.

———. "Leno's Guests." *USA Today,* Apr. 16, 1992.

Kalte, Joanmarie. "Meet the Multimillionaire Comic Who Can't Order Room Service." *TV Guide,* June 10, 1989.

Kaplan, Peter W., and Peter Stevenson. "Wipe That Smirk Off Your Face." *Esquire,* Sept. 1991.

Karlen, Neal. "Stand-up Guy." *Rolling Stone,* July 3, 1986.

Karr, Albert R. "Column." *Wall Street Journal,* Dec. 14, 1991.

Kart, Larry. "Leno's Brand of Modern Comedy Stands Up to the Test of Time." *Chicago Tribune,* Oct. 13, 1985.

Kaufman, Joan, and Michael Alexander. "Profile (Whew!) of a Funny Man." *People,* Nov. 30, 1987.

Kennedy, Dana. "Jay Leno Says He's Still a 'Journeyman Comic.'" *Associated Press,* Jan. 4, 1988.

Kerr, Bob. "Carson Show Just a Break from the Road." *Providence Journal,* Nov. 8, 1987.

Kogan, Rick. "Some Ideas for Leno to Sleep On." *Chicago Tribune,* June 27, 1991.

Kornheiser, Tony. "Stand Up and Be Comic; Jay Leno Rolls into Town with His Late-Night Laugh Track." *Washington Post,* Sept. 24, 1985.

Kubasik, Ben. "Marsalis Set with Leno." *Newsday,* Mar. 10, 1992.

LaSalle, Mike. "Jay Leno Live—Well, Almost; Slick Comedy Routine by a Smooth Operator." *San Francisco Chronicle,* July 27, 1991.

Leno, Jay. "So, You Want to Ride a Motorcycle." *Parade,* Apr. 5, 1992.

Leno, Jay. *Headlines.* New York: Warner Books, 1989.

———. *More Headlines.* New York: Warner Books, 1990.

———. *Headlines III: Not the Movie, Still the Book.* New York: Warner Books, 1991.

Leno, Jay, and Michael Alexander. "Doing Stand-up in the Sand, Comedian Jay Leno Scores a Direct Hit in Saudi Arabia." *People,* Dec. 24, 1990.

Leno, Jay, and Peter Frey. "Runts of the Liter; Small Cars Evaluation, Evaluation." *Playboy,* Apr. 1988.

"Leno Makes Bush's Day." *Associated Press,* Dec. 13, 1991.

"Leno Recalls Meeting Lucille Ball." *Los Angeles Times,* Dec. 8, 1989.

"Leno the Hope of the Nineties?" *United Press International,* Sept. 7, 1990.

"Leno to Entertain Troops in Gulf." *Los Angeles Times,* Sept. 6, 1990.

Lewis, Randy. "Would That Jay Leno's Polish Rubs Off on Other Comics." *Los Angeles Times,* Feb. 7, 1988.

Lieberman, David. "Candidates Roll with the Punch Lines." *New York Times,* Apr. 19, 1992.

Lochte, Dick. "Playboy Interview: Jay Leno." *Playboy*, Dec. 1990.

Lorando, Mark. "Leno on the Road." *New Orleans Times-Picayune*, July 17, 1991.

Margulies, Lee. "Weekend TV: Comic Leno Takes It on the Chin." *Los Angeles Times*, Nov. 1, 1986.

Markovich, Bob. "Everybody's Doing It." *Home Mechanix*, Feb. 1990.

Marx, Andy. "Look What We Found: Stupid Squirrel, You Thought We Were Dead." *Los Angeles Times*, Apr. 12, 1992.

McCallum, Jack. "Next to David Letterman, No One Is More at Home Than Jay Leno, the Stand-up Comic Who's Not Standing Still." *People*, May 19, 1986.

McCollister, John. "The Fastest Comic on Two Wheels." *Saturday Evening Post*, Mar. 1988.

McFarlin, Jim. "Heeeeeeere's . . . Jay!" *Detroit News and Free Press*, July 20, 1991.

"Mean Isn't Funny, Leno Says." *Los Angeles Times*, Jan. 28, 1991.

Mikia, Pete. "He's on the Road Again and Again." *Las Vegas Review Journal*, Jan. 8, 1987.

Mills, David. "No Kidding, Hip Comic Hits It Big." *Washington Times*, Sept. 10, 1986.

Mitchell, Elvis. "Jay Leno." *Fresno Bee*, Jan. 3, 1988.

Morse, Rob. "Leno: Stand-up Guy." *San Francisco Examiner*, July 26, 1991.

O'Connor, John J. "'Jay Leno Special,' Tonight at 11:30 on NBC." *New York Times*, Nov. 1, 1986.

———. "Subtle Changes in Jay Leno's 'Tonight Show." *New York Times*, May 27, 1992.

Orin, Deborah. "President Collects Anti-Mario Jokes from the Expert." *New York Post*, Dec. 13, 1991.

Parks, Steve. "Leno's Quicker Picker-Uppers." *Newsday*, June 24, 1991.

Piccoli, Sean. "The King of Comedy; Jay Leno: Laugh All You Want, He'll Make More." *Washington Times*, June 28, 1991.

———. "The Funniest Man in Stand-up." *Insight on the News*, July 22, 1991.

Price, Hardy. "Comedian Leno Loses Grace Visiting 'Tacky' Elvis Mansion." *Phoenix Arizona Republic*, Mar. 8, 1987.

Protzman, Bob. "Leno's Work Lots of Fun." *St. Paul Pioneer Press-Dispatch*, Sept. 24, 1987.

Radel, Cliff. "Same Jay Leno, But on a Roll with Classy Act." *Cincinnati Enquirer*, Mar. 12, 1987.

Reidy, Chris, and Susan Bickelhaupt. "Jay Leno: He'll Give 'Tonight' Political Bite." *Boston Globe*, June 21, 1991.

Richelieu, David Anthony. "Credibility, Timeliness Keys to Leno's Success." *San Antonio Express News*, Aug. 26, 1990.

Rivers, Scott. "Jay Leno Brings Polished Humor to Symphony Hall." *Salt Lake City Times*, Mar. 8, 1991.

Rosenthal, Andrew. "Leno Finds the Right Lines." *New York Times,* Dec. 13, 1991.

Rosenthal, David N. "Let Leno Sit behind the 'Tonight' Desk—Not Letterman." *Seattle Times,* June 3, 1991.

Scarupa, Henry. "Comedy's Good Guy Prefers to Go for the Jocular." *Baltimore Sun,* June 13, 1989.

Schreiberg, Stu. "He-e-e-e-e-e-r-e's Jay Leno!" *Cosmopolitan,* Sept. 1989.

Scott, Vernon. "Comedian Jay Leno: 'Our Audiences Resent Jokes.'" *United Press International,* Aug. 15, 1983.

Shales, Tom. "Not Ready for Late Night; On NBC Jay Leno's So-So Show." *Washington Post,* Nov. 1, 1986.

———. "Jay Leno and the Constant Comedy; All over the Tube, It's High Hilarity." *Washington Post,* Apr. 11, 1987.

———. "Jay Leno Named Johnny's Successor; Letterman Said to Be 'Furious' over NBC's 'Tonight Show' Pick." *Washington Post,* June 7, 1991.

———. "Jay Leno, Laughing Last; The Comedian's Bumpy Road to the Top of 'Tonight.'" *Washington Post,* June 27, 1991.

Shindler, Merrill. "Cover Q & A: Jay Leno." *Los Angeles Magazine,* Aug. 1989.

"Show for the Jobless." *Stamford* (Conn.) *Advocate,* Jan. 24, 1992.

Siskel, Gene. "Comic Jay Takes a Big Step to the Silver Screen." *Chicago Tribune,* July 19, 1987.

Smith, Mark Chalon. "Leno Pokes Fun with Gentlest Jabs." *Los Angeles Times,* Feb. 18, 1991.

Smith, Steve. "Jay Leno Brings Old-fashioned Comedy Back in Style." *Dallas Times Herald,* Sept. 13, 1987.

Snider, Eric. "Jay Leno." *St. Petersburg Times,* Nov. 30, 1984.

Snyder, Graham. "One for the Road." *Fort Worth Star Telegram,* Sept. 17, 1987.

"Some Enchanted Evenings." *People,* Feb. 17, 1991.

Squitieri, Tom. "Comedian Jay Leno Enlists in USO Show." *USA Today,* Sept. 7, 1990.

Stedman, Nancy. "Comic Jay Leno Is a Credit to His Family." *New York Daily News,* Nov. 22, 1987.

Stengel, Richard. "Midnight's Mayor." *Time,* Mar. 16, 1992.

Suber, Art. "Leno Just a Travelin' Funny Man." *Panama City* (Fla.) *News-Herald.* Mar. 13, 1987.

Swan, Tony. "Recycles." *Popular Mechanics,* Aug. 1988.

Swet, Peter. "Who's That Funny Guy with the Wrench?" *Parade,* Aug. 26, 1990.

Tauber, Peter. "Jay Leno: Not Just Another Funny Face." *New York Times Magazine,* Feb. 26, 1989.

Terhune, Linda. "Jeez!" *Colorado Springs Gazette Telegraph,* Sept. 28, 1990.

Terry, Clifford. "'American Dream': Mom, Cars, and Leno." *Chicago Tribune,* May 2, 1986.

Thompson, John. Letter to editor. *Los Angeles Times,* Nov. 5, 1989.

"Today's 'Tonight' Day for Jay Leno." *Associated Press,* June 6, 1991.

Tucker, Jennifer. "Leno's One-liners Fire His Personal Wars; He's Funny, Clean, and King of Comics." *Tampa Tribune,* Oct. 15, 1989.

"Two Minutes with the Funniest Man in America." *Boston Magazine,* May 2, 1986.

Voss, Melinda. "Jay Leno Can Laugh at Success." *Des Moines Register,* Aug. 21, 1986.

WABC-TV. "Barbara Walters, Legends: The New Generation." *Radio TV Reports,* May 12, 1992.

Waldron, Clarence. "Branford Marsalis and Jay Leno Give 'Tonight Show' New Humor and New Sound." *Jet,* June 22, 1992.

Warren, Jill. "Setting Means Less to Comic Than Response." *Indianapolis Star,* Feb. 2, 1986.

WCBS-TV. "60 Minutes." *Radio TV Reports,* Mar. 15, 1992.

Wells, Paul. "He-e-e-ere's Branford: Marsalis Joins Leno." *Montreal Gazette.* Dec. 17, 1991.

Whearley, Jay. "Hard-Working Comedian Tells Them as He Sees Them." *Denver Post,* Mar. 16, 1986.

Williams, Jeannie. "Jay Leno: The Tonight Show." *USA Today,* June 26, 1991.

Williams, Stephen. "Jay Leno, Mr. Goodjoke." *Newsday,* Apr. 2, 1989.

WNBC-TV. "Late Night with David Letterman." *Radio TV Reports,* Dec. 12, 1991.

WNBC-TV. "Later with Bob Costas." *Radio TV Reports,* May 20/21, 1992.

WNBC-TV. "Today." *Radio TV Reports,* May 25/26, 1992.

Wolcott, James. "The Fears of a Clown." *Vanity Fair,* July 1991.

Wood, Tom. "Jay Leno Gets a Kick out of Comedy." *Nashville Tennessean,* Mar. 3, 1984.

Woodard, Josef. "He's a Diehard of Club, Concert Circuit Working a Good 300 Nights a Year." *Santa Barbara News-Press,* Jan. 24, 1987.

Worner, Alka. "NBC Picks Jay Leno to Succeed Johnny Carson." *United Press International,* June 6, 1991.

Zehme, Bill. "20 Questions: Jay Leno." *Playboy,* Jan. 1986.

———. "A Stand-up Kind of Guy." *Playboy,* July 1988.

Zoglin, Richard. "And What a Reign It Was." *Time,* Mar. 16, 1992.

Zoglin, Richard, Kathleen Brady, and Elaine Dutka. "Stand-up Comedy on a Roll." *Time,* Aug. 24, 1987.